FUNNY BONES

WRITTEN AND ILLUSTRATED BY
DR. DAVID FRIEDMAN

PRAISE AND GIGGLES FOR
FUNNY BONES

"This is the absolute funniest book ever written in the history of mankind! I'm proud of the author for writing it, but I'd be a lot happier if he called me more."

—**Gail Friedman**, David's mother

"I'm a clown who is a doctor, not a doctor who is a clown. I loved the silly stories in *Funny Bones*!"

—**Patch Adams**, MD

"Everyone needs more laughter. It truly is good for the soul! And this book made me smile, chuckle, and laugh out loud on every page. I promise it will do the same for you."

—**Jack Canfield**, author of the #1 *New York Times* bestselling *Chicken Soup for the Soul*® series

"*Funny Bones* made me laugh so hard I almost cracked a rib! Dr. Friedman is the doctor I always wanted to have. His wild and wacky stories are right up my alley!"

—**Renée Taylor**, comedian, Oscar-nominated, Emmy Award–winning actress

"Laughter really is the best medicine, unless you've had massive organ failure. With so many stuffy, stern, and glum doctors, kudos to Dr. Friedman for creating some needed smiles in his clinic and around the world. Laughter helps get us through tough times. Even if you've been divorced four times and lost all your money to alimony, your house, and everything; just being able to laugh about it can help pull you through like nothing else."

—**Tom Arnold**, actor, comedian, and comedy writer

"Congrats to Dr. Friedman for his new book *Funny Bones*. I may be America's favorite pothead, but he is a bone-afide crackhead! The last time I had my back cracked, I felt so good it was as if I smoked a chiropractic doobie! Keep up the great spine-tingling smiles and chuckles."

—**Tommy Chong**, comedian ("Cheech & Chong,"), actor, and cannabis activist

"I don't know what a comedy book is worth, so I called a buddy of mine who's an LOL professional. He appraised Dr. Friedman's book *Funny Bones* and said it is indeed genuine and worth a million laughs."

—**Rick Harrison**, star of the award-winning TV series *Pawn Stars*

"I laughed so hard reading *Funny Bones*, part of the French fry I was eating came shooting out of my nose! The last chiropractor I went to pushed so hard on my back, he squashed my balls, and that's why I talk with this high pitch voice."

—**High Pitch Erik**, comedian, the *Howard Stern Show*

"There are many ways to cope with stress. Maybe you listen to music or go for a massage. I go see a chiropractor. Often times when I'm on the treatment table, I tell him things I would not tell the average person. Wouldn't it be crazy if a chiropractor documented those stories and recorded them in a book of hilarity? Dr. Friedman has done it! *Funny Bones* is the ultimate prescription for what ails you. It's a must-read for anyone that wants to escape their stressed-out, worrisome, and depressing lives! If you want a good laugh and a great read, *Funny Bones* is the book for you!"

—**Brad Williams**, stand-up comic, Netflix's *The Degenerates*, Showtime, Comedy Central

"I highly commend Dr. Friedman for bringing some needed puns, wit, and humor to the world. It's been said that comedians live the longest lives because we laugh, and I think the last couple of years have shown us how important laughter is. It really is the best anti-aging tool, and Dr. Friedman is helping people live longer. Due to all my comedy, I'm 141 years old (and moisturized). Thank you, Dr. Friedman, for keeping the populous youthful."

—**Colin Mochrie**, international comedy icon, actor, producer, and star of *Whose Line Is It Anyway?*

"Chiropractors love me because my right hook has sent many of my opponents to see one. I am the king of punches, but Dr. Friedman is the king of punchlines! My uppercut has knocked the smile off of many faces and his cutting up has created smiling faces."

—**Larry Holmes**, heavyweight boxing champion and International Boxing Hall of Fame inductee

"Finally, a doctor who puts the needs of his patients first. Unlike urologists whose receptionists always answer the phone with, 'Can you hold please?' or dermatologists who constantly make rash decisions, Dr. Friedman offers a message of hope and healing, with lots of laughter in between."

—**Gilbert Gottfried**, stand-up comedian, actor

"Warning: Don't read *Funny Bones* with a full bladder! You'll pee in your pants and have to do laundry."

—**Stan Lawrence**, stand-up comedian, Comedy Central presents, Showtime at the Apollo

"I've met a chiropractor or two in my lifetime and the fact that Dr. Friedman is hysterical, entertains his patients, and wrote a book about it means that he is pretty darn cool!"

—**James "Murr" Murray**, comedian, star of the hit television show *Impractical Jokers*

"With so much stress and craziness in this world, WE'RE NOT GONNA TAKE IT ANYMORE! There's just one thing left to do: I WANNA LAUGH! It's great seeing twisted humor coming from a twisted doctor that twists people's backs for a living. The greatest cure for everything is laughter and, of course, a good chiropractic visit helps too. You are doing God's work, Dr. Friedman."

—**Dee Snider**, lead singer of the platinum award-winning rock band Twisted Sister

"Music feeds the soul, but laughter empowers the body. Dr. Friedman's book *Funny Bones* will give you a good belly laugh! A lot of musicians, including me, rely on chiropractic care and I applaud him for adding humor between all the snaps, crackles, and pops."

—**Arnel Pineda**, lead singer of Journey and Rock & Roll Hall of Fame inductee

"*Funny Bones* will give you such a belly laugh, you'll feel like you did a hundred crunches. Dr. Friedman has given all you lazy bums the perfect excuse not to exercise! Each chapter has so many KILLER jokes, you may end up dying from laughter."

—**Ben Price**, impressionist, *AGT* grand finalist, *The Today Show*, *The Morning Show*, NBC, Fox, and more

"*Funny Bones* is a hilarious book that bares it all and uncovers what really goes on behind closed doors at a chiropractor's office."

—**Mr. Uekusa** (aka "The Naked Comedian"), *France's* and *Britain's Got Talent* finalist

"Laughter is one of life's best natural medications. When you laugh, your brain releases a cascade of neurochemicals resulting in mirth and feelings of well-being. It might even contribute to longevity. *Funny Bones* is a highly readable dose of humor, packed with clinical stories that will delight."

—**Dr. Drew Pinsky**, addiction medicine specialist, star of *Dr. Drew on Call*, *Celebrity Rahab*, and host of the syndicated radio talk show *Loveline*

"When someone laughs, it lowers blood pressure, oxygenates the blood, and improves vascular function. *Funny Bones* is a must-read if you want to decrease your risk of having a heart attack."

—Dr. **Stephen Sinatra**, bestselling author, world-renowned cardiologist, and founder of the New England Heart Center

"Laughter is the ultimate anti-aging solution. It increases human growth hormone and reduces cortisol, the skin wrinkling, belly-fat producing stress hormone. *Funny Bones* is going to put me out of business!"

—Dr. **Anthony Youn**, award-winning author and anti-aging expert, voted best plastic surgeon by *US News & World Report* and *Harper's Bazaar*

"Dr. David Friedman is masterful in combining his sharp wit, playful sense of humor, and intelligence with the insights gleaned throughout his three-decade career in the chiropractic field. Each chapter of *Funny Bones* contains gems that will elicit spontaneous emotional laughter, ensuring the reader enjoys plenty of feel-good endorphins and helping to alleviate stress, calm the mind, and uplift the spirit!"

—Dr. **Kristen Willeumier**, neuroscientist and bestselling author of *Biohack Your Brain*

"Laughter truly is the best medicine. A good, deep belly laugh activates the vagus nerve, which supports better digestion, a healthy gut lining, and organ function. Let *Funny Bones* give you a happy belly laugh, just like it did me!"

—**Vincent Pedre**, MD, FMCP, author of the bestseller *Happy Gut: The Cleansing Program to Help You Lose Weight, Gain Energy, and Eliminate Pain*

ALSO BY
DR. DAVID FRIEDMAN

Food Sanity: How to Eat in a World of Fads and Fiction

A Cup of Coffee with 10 Leading Chiropractors in the United States

Understanding the Nervous System

DR. DAVID FRIEDMAN

FUNNY BONES

TRUE TALES FROM A CHIROPRACTOR THAT WILL CRACK YOU UP!

RIVER GROVE
BOOKS

Published by River Grove Books
Austin, TX
www.rivergrovebooks.com

Distributed by River Grove Books

Design and composition by Greenleaf Book Group and Brian Phillips
Cover design by Greenleaf Book Group and Brian Phillips

Publisher's Cataloging-in-Publication data is available.

Print ISBN: 978-1-63299-617-6

eBook ISBN: 978-1-63299-618-3

First Edition

CONTENTS

INTRODUCTION

YOU'VE PROBABLY HEARD THE POPULAR SAYING, "Laughter is the best form of medicine." There's actual research to back this up. According to the *Journal of Neuroscience*, laughter releases endorphins in the brain via opioid receptors. Similar to addictive narcotic drugs like heroin, which also bind to those receptors, laughter induces euphoria, minus the negative side effects. Laughter also activates the release of serotonin, the key hormone that stabilizes our mood, feelings of well-being, and happiness. A good belly laugh also increases our number of immune cells and infection-fighting antibodies.[1]

That will be the one and only reference to any scientific literature you will see in this book. In my international award-winning, number-one bestselling book, *Food Sanity: How to Eat in a World of Fads and Fiction*, I shared more than a thousand references. The book I wrote prior to that one was a college textbook on neuroanatomy. Both of these books covered some serious topics and included many scientific studies. Not this time. Not this book!

For the record, I do not have any formal education in making people laugh. I did not earn any degree or certification in comedy, nor did I complete an LOL internship. In fact, as a clinician and syndicated TV and radio health expert, I've dealt with some pretty *serious* health topics, ranging from spinal stenosis and diabetes to arthritis, heart disease, and cancer. My education includes doctor of chiropractic, doctor of naturopathy, and a post-doctorate certification in neurology. I'm also a board-certified integrative and alternative medical practitioner.

---

1   Sandra Manninen et al., "Social Laughter Triggers Endogenous Opioid Release in Humans," *Journal of Neuroscience* 37, no. 25 (June 2017): 6125–31.

Although I wear several serious hats, I still make it a habit to find humor in every aspect of my life. Being a holistic doctor, I don't perform surgery; however, my patients tell me quite often that I leave them in stitches. Over the years, many people have recommended that I quit my day job and become a stand-up comedian. That makes sense considering I'm short in stature and if I weren't *standing up*, no one would see me on stage.

Mark Twain once said, "The truth is stranger than fiction," and this book is proof of that! The stories I share are *true events* that actually took place in my clinic (only the names have been changed to protect the hilarious).

As a chiropractor, I've spent over three decades literally *talking behind my patients' backs*. With my advanced training in neurology, it's quite common to find me *getting on my patients' nerves*. In addition, my knowledge of diet and nutrition allows me to share useful *feed*back regarding patients' eating habits. But with this book, I can finally take off my tie, step away from all the nerdy scientific talk, and focus on just one part of the human anatomy: the funny bone.

Even though I am supposed to undo knots, I like to twist things up once in a while with brain teasers that either entertain or simply keep a patient's mind off the pain they are experiencing. It's not uncommon for people, especially those new to chiropractic, to be on edge, not knowing what to expect. So, I like to disengage their anxiety using a little laughter. Over the years, I've been blessed to have treated many patients who have a great sense of humor, too. So, from puns and wisecracks to practical jokes on both sides of the treatment table, you'll find it all here.

I'm originally from up north (yep, I'm a Yankee), and after moving to a quaint little town in North Carolina and setting up a practice, I had to get accustomed to how southerners talk. While I've grown used to it now, for a few years it was truly a foreign language to me and resulted in some funny misunderstandings, several of which I'll share with you in this book.

I live in Wilmington, NC, which is often called "Filmington" because so many movies are filmed here. I treat a lot of celebrities in my office, on the set, and in other locations. The *Hollywood Reporter* has even called me "The Chiropractor to the Stars." A few of my notable patients have included John Travolta, Jenny McCarthy, Patrick Swayze, Anthony Hopkins, and Paul Newman. I will share a few of the humorous interactions I've had with some of Hollywood's elite.

I'm a "word nerd," and some of the humor in this book will be a play on words. If by some chance you read a pun, joke, or witty comment that you don't quite grasp, try saying the sentence out loud. Sometimes hearing it will create an *aha* and *haha* moment. Feel free to flip through this book at your leisure or read it straight through. If you pull a muscle or strain a joint from laughing too hard, call me. I'll fix it.

DISCLAIMER: I've never laughed at anyone in my office, but I have laughed *with them*. People have become more sensitive lately and since some of the humor in this book spans three decades, I made a *snap decision* to hire a young editor to delete any content that may possibly *rub you the wrong way*. However, that being a subjective task, I hope what remains will help to loosen up your pressure points and give you a brief escape from life's spasms and existential daily headaches.

THE X-RAY CONFIRMS MY DIAGNOSIS.
YOU HAVE A TWISTED SENSE OF HUMOR.

PUN-CHLINES AND WIT

I'M A BIG FAN OF WORDPLAY. SO MUCH SO, that when the doctor confirmed my mom was pregnant, he told her that she had a *pun* in the oven. Since then, I've *groan* up to live by the mantra, "Seven days without a pun makes one *weak*." Besides, everyone seems to love a good pun, except for kleptomaniacs—they're always taking things *literally*. Here's some improvisational wit, puns, and sarcasm from my clinic.

Patient: I'm about to have surgery next month unless you can fix me. Can you perform under pressure?

Me: I don't know that one, but I can sing "Bohemian Rhapsody."

Patient: I do not want a doctor delivering my baby. I prefer a midwife but none of them in town are accepting new patients.

Me: It sounds like you're having a midwife crisis.

Patient: My back is killing me after kayaking. Do you think you can help me?

Me: Of course I can. I'm a *kayak*practor.

Me: Anything new bothering you?

Patient: No, nothing major.

Me: I appreciate the respect, but I'm just a corporal.

I was going over my findings with a patient who was from Germany. The topic of diet came up and he mentioned that he consumes a lot of meat, especially sausage. I told him I already knew that from looking at his X-ray.

"You can tell I eat sausage from my X-ray?" he asked with a puzzled look on his face.

"Yes, with X-rays I can see the wurst in people."

Patient: My foot feels like it's asleep.

Me: It's outright coma toes!

Patient: I wanted you to see my husband today, but your receptionist told me he has to wait until tomorrow.

Me: Sorry, but I'm scheduled back-to-back all day!

Me: What seems to be your trouble?

Patient: Every morning when I get up, I feel dizzy for one hour.

Me: Try getting up one hour later.

A woman came to see me after hurting her back while lifting a heavy bag of garbage. As I was treating her, I shared the proper way to lift so that it wouldn't happen again. She came back a while later with the same problem caused by lifting a heavy bag of garbage. As she lay face down on the treatment table, I reminded her of the best way to lift something without hurting her back. Then it suddenly occurred to me, and I said, "Oh my God! Here I am once again talking trash behind your back!"

A patient counts off her chronic ailments on her fingers: "Doc, I have back pain, headaches, bad sinus infections, and ringing of the ears. Is there any good news you can share with me?"

"Yes, look on the bright side. On one hand, you have back pain, headaches, sinus infections, and ringing of the ears. On the other hand, you have five good fingers."

After a lapse in her appointments, a patient admitted, "I've been putting this off for nine months!"

I replied, "That's what my mother said the day I was born!"

Patient: I previously broke my back in two places.

Me: Stop going to those places.

Patient: Dr. Friedman, you have great hands. You should be a masseuse.

Me: That's why they call me *Doctor Seuss*.

A nervous new arrival asked with much concern, "You are twisting and cracking the spine, which is right next to the brainstem, spinal cord, arteries, veins, and nerves. How well do you know the anatomy and what's your confidence level that you won't cause damage when you pop someone's spine?"

"Rest assured," I replied. "I've been working on patients for over thirty years, and I know the spine like I know the back of my hand!"

To prove my point, I glanced at the back of my hand, pointed to my knuckles, and jokingly said, "What the heck are these?"

Patient: My eyes are so sore after reading all weekend.

Me: What did you read, a giraffe pop-up book?

"Doc, I have a really bad head cold. I can hardly breathe," my patient, Michelle, told me.

"It's all in your head!" I reassured her.

"No, it's not! I *really* do have a head cold!" she exclaimed.

"And I'm telling you, Michelle, that it's all in your head!" I insisted.

"No, I really do have a head cold!"

We could have gone on like that for hours, but she finally got it and laughed.

....

Patient: Ever since I gave birth three years ago, I've been suffering from sinus issues. What do you think it is?

Me: Postnatal drip.

....

What do you call a patient who goes without treatment for a long period of time?

Crack-a-lackin'.

....

While doing a consultation, a man looked at the anatomy chart on the wall and said, "I see there's a nerve coming from the neck that goes to the heart."

I replied, "Yes, it's called the vagus nerve. It's what innervates the heart."

"So, for people with heart issues, what happens when you unpinch that nerve in the neck?"

"I'm sorry," I replied, "I can't tell you that."

He gave me a puzzled look and asked, "Why?"

"Because what happens in the vagus nerve stays in the vagus nerve."

....

Patient: I haven't slept for ten days!

Me: Good. Because that's way too long.

I felt a patient's back and asked, "Did you go swimming this morning?"

"Yes, I did," she replied. "How on earth could you tell that from my spine?"

I replied, "Just like Spider-Man has *Spidey Sense*, I have *Spiney Sense*."

(Actually, the scent of chlorine on her body gave it away.)

Patient: I hurt my back while building a shed in my backyard.

Me: Are you shedding me?

Patient: No, I really did.

Me: Oh well, shed happens.

Patient: You really think you can help me?

Me: I'll take a crack at it.

An upset patient scheduled a consultation to speak with me. I walked into the room, and he said, "Doc, I've got a bone to pick with you! You told me when I first came to see you that in ten weeks I would be fixed and pain-free! That was *three months* ago, and I'm just as bad today, if not worse, than the day I first came in."

Scratching my head, I looked at his chart. Realization dawned, and I replied, "Yes, I did say that you would be fixed in ten weeks; however, I haven't seen you since your first appointment. Correcting your spine requires actually coming in for treatments during those ten weeks."

Patient: I love the soothing music you play in the office. It's so relaxing.

Me: Me too. Most chiropractors just listen to hip-pop.

Me: What are you doing after your treatment?

Patient: I left work to come here, and I'm going straight back.

Me: Yes, you are.

Patient: Dr. Friedman, my headache was so bad over the weekend that the only relief I could get was from leaning against the wall and rolling my neck on two tennis balls.

Me: That's called a *balls-to-the-wall* headache!

"I heard you work on carpel tunnel syndrome. Can you please check my wrist?" a patient asked.

I took out a pen and wrote a checkmark on his wrist.

He gave me a puzzled look and said, "Why did you do that?"

"You asked me to *check* your wrist."

He laughed and said, "No, I want you to *evaluate* and *treat* my wrist."

A carpenter needed treatment after he strained his lower back picking up heavy wood.

Diagnosis: he hurt his lumbar lifting lumber.

Me: Did you hear about corduroy pillows? They're making headlines this week!

Patient: No, I didn't hear about that. Why are they making headlines?

Me: Because people are lying on them.

Patient: And that's making headlines?

Me: Yes, lying on corduroy pillows makes *head lines*.

Patient: I was in a bad mood when I got here, but after your treatment, I'm happy again.

Me: That's because I specialize in attitude adjustments.

Patient: Doc, will this treatment hurt?

Me: It won't hurt me at all, but I appreciate your concern for my well-being.

Patient: Before you, both my hips hurt so bad I couldn't walk. Now they feel great!

Me: Hip hip, hooray!

Patient: My wife told me to come see you so I would have a better future.

Me: Yes, your back problems are all behind you.

A patient climbed up on the table and said, "Before you do your adjustment today, please watch the knee. I just had surgery on it."

I stared at her knee until, a good thirty seconds later, my patient asked, "What are you doing?"

I replied, "You told me to watch your knee."

Noticing dried egg yolk on a patient's shirt, I decided to play my psychic abilities trick and said, "I bet I can tell you what you had for breakfast this morning."

"Okay, Doc, what did I eat for breakfast?"

"You had eggs."

"Nope, I had eggs for breakfast yesterday."

(I didn't tell him about the dried egg yolk and just let him think I wasn't psychic after all.)

Patient: I have a huge hemorrhoid so please be careful when you twist and push on me.

Me: You think you have a big hemorrhoid? I once had a patient come in with a hemorrhoid so gigantic that it touched his thigh. This is called a thyroid.

I've always wondered, why aren't hemorrhoids called assteroids?

Patient: I have chronic pain in my feet and numbness in my toes.

Me: The next time you are feeling *de-feeted*, call a *toe truck* to come to your rescue!

There's a restaurant right next to my office, and the owner, Kathy, is a regular patient.

"You're here so much, we should combine our businesses," I suggested one day. "We can call it Wilmington's Crack & Snack Center."

I'm often called to work on the cast and crew of television shows and movies.

On one movie set, the only place they had for me to set up my portable treatment table was next to craft services, where they offer beverages, food, and snacks.

One day, the craft service director was out sick, so I told them that I could just do both jobs since my table was set up next to craft services. I could treat patients between handing out food. I even came up with a name for my new business: Crepes & Scrapes.

My long-time patient, Joe, came in to see me with back pain. As I was doing deep muscle work on him, he shouted, "I can't believe I'm spending my hard-earned money on this torture!" and I replied, "The torture is free. I only charge you for the jokes."

Patient: My back hurts. I slept funny last night.

Me: I'm jealous. I could use a good laugh at night after a long day at work.

Patient: Dr. Friedman, I feel great. You are truly outstanding in your field!

Me: Nope, I've been indoors all day.

Ann was pondering the cause of her back pain. "I have a feeling it's from hunching over my desk at work," she said.
    I replied, "I have a hunch you're right."

Patient: I've got a crook in my neck!

Me: Did it rob a bank?!

A popular phrase in the South is "My back is as sore as a risen." I never learned that term in chiropractic college, so the first time one of my patients made such a complaint, I googled it. Turns out, a *risen* is a boil, which is a very painful, pus-filled bump on the skin. Next time, I planned to ask someone who presented with a "back that's as sore as a risen," why they didn't just say, "My back is as sore as a zit that needs popping"?

Patient: You work on Frank Myers. He's my cousin, twice removed.

Me: Does that mean you unfriended Frank twice on Facebook?

An enormous bodybuilder came in one day with such tight muscles that I had to work overtime on him. After I was finished, I said, "You got me sweating so much, you just made my Right Guard go left!"

A patient came in with severe low back pain after bending over and cleaning out stalls where she kept her horses.

I adjusted her back and as I was walking her to the therapy room, her husband saw me in the hallway and asked how his wife was doing.

I replied, "Her condition is *stable*."

A man came to see me with a dislocated shoulder and asked me if I could fix it. I replied, "I'm going to treat your shoulder like the Ronco Rotisserie infomercial: I'll just *set it and you can forget it!*"

After we went from standard X-ray to digital, there was a learning curve on figuring out how to work the software to analyze X-rays. The tool I needed the most was the pointer so that I could show patients exactly where their problem area was.

My office manager tried to help me figure out how to make the pointer work—to no avail. After an hour of getting nowhere, I said, "Well, all that time spent was really *point* less!"

Patient: You stay so busy, Dr. Friedman. How do you keep up?

Me: Sometimes it's not easy doing it all myself.

Patient: Too bad you can't clone yourself.

Me: If I was able to clone myself, I would probably open a men's fragrance line and call it . . . *Clone's Cologne.*

Patient: I keep peeing a lot, and my doctor told me it's because the urethra is no longer working.

Me: He's wrong. *The* Aretha is working. In fact, Aretha Franklin is out on tour this year.

Patient: I said *uretha*, not Aretha.

Me: Oh, I'm sorry for the misunderstanding. I hope you didn't lose too much R-E-S-P-E-C-T for me.

A new patient came in, and during her first treatment, I said, "Heather, this is the absolute worst I've ever seen your back!"

She said, "OMG! That's awful. Why do you think it's the worst you've ever seen me?"

I replied, "Because today's your very first appointment."

I was adjusting someone's neck, and it was barely out of place.

The patient said, "That was just a mini clunk."

I replied, "Most of the time you need a maxi clunk."

She laughed and said, "The sounds like a feminine hygiene product."

Patient: My medical doctor said I need to get a cortisone shot, but my coworker said he had the same thing and you fixed him after just a few treatments.

Me: Yes, you have a common condition that I have had great results with.

Patient: Okay, I'm giving it a shot!

Me: I don't think that's a good idea.

Patient: But I thought you said you could help me.

Me: Yes, I can, which is why I don't recommend you give it a shot!

Patient: My right leg pain wakes me up at night. What can I do?

Me: Press on your kneecap, and you'll get nine more minutes of sleep.

Patient: And what happens when it wakes me up again?

Me: Do it again, and you'll get another nine minutes. It's a snooze pressure point.

As I was doing trigger point therapy on a patient's pinched sciatic nerve, she grimaced, and I said, "You didn't know I would be getting on your nerves today, did you?"

Patient: You put in a lot of hours, Dr. Friedman.

Me: That's okay. Chiropractors get back pay.

Patient: I don't think there's anything left for you to work on; while I was waiting for you on the chair, I twisted and felt a giant crack.

Me: (walking over to the chair) I don't see it.

Patient: My back has been out for a long time!

Me: I agree. It feels like it's way-out past curfew.

A woman told me she would have to miss about six weeks of treatments because she was getting her right hip replaced.

"Did you have an injury?" I asked.

She sighed and replied, "No, it's just old age."

"How's your left hip?" I asked.

She said, "Oh, that one is fine."

I gave her a serious look. "Then how can you blame old age? Weren't both of your hips born on the same day? Haven't they walked the exact number of steps?"

A professional artist came in and, after three weeks of treatments, she said, "Before coming to see you, I literally couldn't stand at the canvas to paint due to the excruciating pain. My paintings were a disaster! Now, thanks to you, I can stand at the canvas, and I'm painting better than ever!"

I replied, "I'm glad I could help you turn your *disaster piece* into your *masterpiece.*"

As I was working on a patient and chitchatting, I rolled her on her side and asked, "Are you still doing interior design work?"

She said, "Yes, but I just do it on the side."

I replied, "So you're doing it right now?"

Patient: I have a lot of back issues.

Me: You should throw those back issues in the trash and cancel subscriptions to future issues.

Patient: Dr. Friedman, I'm so impressed. You write books, host a radio show, appear on TV, formulate nutritional products, and still manage to see patients full-time. You are truly a jack of all trades!

Me: Yes, but when I see you, I'm a Cracker Jack of this trade.

Patient: Is there any way you can treat me without cracking my back?

Me: Can your dentist fix your cavity without using a drill?

Me: Knock, knock.

Patient: Who's there?

Me: HIPAA

Patient: HIPAA who?

Me: Sorry, I'm not allowed to tell you.

A patient said, "My neighbor told me you are funny. Tell me a joke."
I replied, "Do you want to hear an inside joke?"
She smiled and said, "Sure."
So, I closed my mouth and mumbled.
She gave me a confused look and said, "I can't understand what you're saying because you have your mouth closed."
I replied, "That's because it's an inside joke."

A patient came in lacking the ability to move her back and neck. I examined her and gave her my diagnosis: "You are suffering from *less*bility!"
"What's that?" she asked.
I replied, "If mobility means having more ability to move, then you have the opposite which is *less*bility."

A patient gets her first side posture adjustment and shouts, "WOW!"
I reply, "Since you are saying WOW sideways, it's 3-0-3!"

Patient: That's the best adjustment ever! How can you top that today?

Me: I don't think I can. In fact, the best I have to offer any other patient I see today is mediocrity.

After an adjustment, a patient said, "I'm impressed!"
I replied, "You'd be more IMPRESSED if I was a dry-cleaning service."

Patient: I didn't mean to scream and moan last time, but I was in a lot of pain. I did feel much better after the treatment.

Me: I'm glad you are feeling better. I take back all the bad things you said about me.

Patient: My right shoulder hurts when I sleep on my side. Any suggestions?

Me: Yes, always sleep with the bad side up. So, if your right shoulder hurts, sleep on your left side. *Bad side up!*

Patient: I do a lot of yard work. Any suggestions?

Me: Yes. If you're installing sod, it's always *green side up!*

Patient: *What are* some things I can add to my diet to help relieve these tight muscles.

Me: Yes, I agree. *Water!*

Patient: Huh? That's what I'm asking you. What are?

Me: And I'm agreeing with you, *water*.

Patient: I'm confused. *What are* some things I can add to my diet to help relieve these tight muscles?

Me: Yes, I agree. *Water* is the best thing you can add to your diet to help your muscles.

Patient: If you fix me, I promise I won't do anything else stupid!

Me: Okay, but please stop calling me stupid.

I treat people who have been in car accidents, and the majority are from rear-end collisions. In fact, eighty percent of all accidents occur because people drive too close to the car in front of them.

So, in an effort to help keep my patients safe, I had a bumper sticker made that says, "Drive any closer, and we'll both need Friedman Chiropractic!"

Patient: Is there anything I can do to help relieve my tight back muscles?

Me: Yes, you should try knee-toe.

Patient: I already follow a keto diet. It helps me lose weight but does nothing for my back pain.

Me: No, I said knee-toe. Straighten both of your knees and touch your toes. Repeat.

A patient with the last name Heinz came in for treatment right after getting an eye examination.

"Do you need glasses?" I asked.

"No, I have perfect vision," he said.

I replied, "So I guess Heinz sight really is 20-20."

A few weeks later, he came back. My office was really backed up and I was running behind. When I finally got to him, he asked, "Why did you keep me waiting for so long?"

I replied to the tune of the eighties' Heinz Ketchup commercial, "Anticipation was keeping you wai-wai-waitinggg . . . I'm slow good!"

I was working on someone's back and told her, "I found the problem," as I pushed my elbow into the muscle to help relax it.

The patient said, "Great. Can you tell me exactly what it is?"

I replied, "Yes, it's my elbow."

A construction worker came in with severe back pain. He said, "I sure hope you brought your hammer today. My back needs a lot of repairs!"

I replied, "Nope. But if I did have a hammer, do you know what I would do?"

"What?" he asked.

I said, "Hammer in the morning all over this land—just like Peter, Paul and Mary."

A patient of mine was a retired engineer who used to build rockets for NASA.

On his first visit, I was showing him a problem on his X-ray, and he said, "I'm not sure I understand."

I replied, "Geez, this isn't rocket science!"

One day this same retiree from NASA was late for his appointment because of a traffic jam. He told me he was losing his patience with bad drivers and was on the verge of road rage.

I said, "You're becoming a real NASA hole!"

I treat the mayor of my city. When he came in one day for his appointment, I asked him where he was hurting.

He replied, "The right side is fine, but the left sucks!"

I laughed and said, "Spoken like a true Republican!"

In my office, we use color-coded folders to designate what room a patient is in. For example, a yellow folder correlates with the "yellow room," which is our reexamination room.

One day, my assistant was escorting a woman back and said, "Oh, you get the red room today."

The patient smiled and said, "I didn't know Dr. Friedman was into fifty shades of cracking!"

After having heard this, we laughed, and then I told her, "Actually, all of us chiropractors are into S&M—*spinal manipulation*."

Me: Is it true this will be your first chiropractic adjustment?

Patient: Yes, and I'm a little nervous.

Me: Okay, just relax, David. It's just a neck adjustment. Do not panic. You can do this!

Patient: My name is not David.

Me: I know. I'm David. I'm just easing some of my *own* fear.

(Patient looks alarmed.)

Me: Just kidding.

Me: How many chiropractors does it take to screw in a lightbulb?

Patient: I'm not sure. How many?

Me: Just one, but it takes ten visits.

Patient: I'm in so much pain. I really need you!

Me: Your muscles are so tight. I will really knead you!

Patient: Doc, my head feels congested.

Me: Any drainage?

Patient: Just the eyes have it.

Me: All those in favor, say . . . eye!

Me: You've got your follow-up spinal exam next time.

Patient: Is there anything I should do to prepare?

Me: Yes, study for it like you would a blood and urine test, and be sure to bring a number-two pencil with you.

Right after an adjustment, a patient said, "Wow, I really heard that pop!"

I replied, "I'm glad you heard that, but please don't call me Pop. It makes me feel so old."

I see so many patients who are addicted to their electronics, always slouching over their smartphones on social media or while playing games.

When I told one patient that he should try to cut back, he said, "I can't help it. I'm addicted to Twitter. Aren't you?"

I replied, "I'm sorry, but I don't follow."

Patient: I am a classical music composer, and after I stand for hours, I'm in excruciating pain!

Me: It sounds like you have a Bach problem.

Ted came in after sustaining injuries from a fall a year prior. He had sought care from multiple doctors but to no avail.

I examined him and found a tender spot, and he shouted with excitement, "Yes, Doc, you are dead on!"

I replied, "Of corpse I am!"

Patient: I loved your book *Food Sanity*. It was a real page-turner!

Me: Thanks! Many of my patients have also told me that I'm a real head-turner.

A woman came in one day with elbow pain. When I put up her X-rays, I said, "What's a nice joint like this doing in a girl like you?"

On a busy Monday, we had a few emergency patients walk in and we were running behind. The phone rang . . .

Office manager: Friedman Chiropractic, how may I help you?

The person on the phone: Yes, I'd like to make an appointment to see Dr. Friedman?

Office manager: When would you like to see him?

The person on the phone: Thirty minutes ago. I'm still sitting in the treatment room waiting for him to come in and see me.

A patient came in really stiff one day. I said, "Man, you are worse than the Norm!"

"Really?"

"Yeah, the actor George Wendt, Norm on *Cheers*, has nothing on you."

"My knee hurts, and I know it's because I am getting old," a patient told me.

So, I treated his knee. At his next visit, he told me he hadn't felt this good since he was a kid.

I smiled and said, "Well, I guess that means your old adult knee is now your youthful *kid-knee*."

Me: It's time for your X-rays.

Patient: I don't have to take all my clothes off, do I?

Me: No, I produce G-rated films—none are *X-ray*ted.

Patient: I'm taking a lot of pills for my pain and various ailments. I'm hoping you can help me get off of them.

Me: Yes, I see you are taking Tylenol, Atenolol, Metoprolol, and Geritol. I'm going to help you put an End-to-itol.

While testing a patient's knee reflexes, she said, "You seem to really love your job."

I replied, "Yes, I get a kick out of it."

Patient: The left side of my neck hurts and so does my left shoulder, left back, and left leg!

Me: Well, I guess that makes you all right!

While I don't make a habit of it, I will occasionally treat animals, especially if a vet refers the owner to me.

One day a woman brought in her limping dog. I found a carpel bone in his paw that was out, and I reset it.

She asked for the diagnosis, and I told her, "It was *car-paw* tunnel syndrome."

Patient: I always wake up hurting. I'm not sure, but I think I may be sleeping funny.

Me: Maybe you should film yourself tonight and see if you laugh when you watch the video tomorrow morning.

Patient: What's the best thing I can do for my tennis elbow at home?

Me: Ice it for twenty minutes.

Patient: It's too difficult to wrap ice cubes around my elbow.

Me: Then try using a bag of frozen peas.

Patient: You really think that will help?

Me: Come on man, give peas a chance. ✌️

Patient: Okay, Doc, go easy on me. You don't have to use so much pressure. How about if I give you my name, rank, and serial number before we start!

Me: I'm glad you decided to talk! We chiropractors make great interrogators because our patients always crack under pressure.

Patient: Thanks for doing such a wonderful job taking care of me for all these years!

Me: Have no fear, I've always got your back.

I was doing some soft tissue massage on a patient, and she said, "That feels great! I wish you could do that for an hour!"

I replied, "No problem. I'll give you an entire hour if you want."

She smiled and said, "Wow! Really?!"

"Yes," I replied, "in sixty-second increments. Starting the next time I see you, you'll have fifty-nine minutes remaining."

Roxanne, a patient who suffers from allergies, said, "Every year I get so sick from all the pollen."

I replied, "Just get a box of Ritz and give pollen what pollen wants, and you should be okay."

Roxanne asked, "What does pollen want?"

I replied, "Pollen wants a cracker."

Patient: My shoulder is killing me. Can you please check it out?

Me: I can't check it out. I forgot my library card.

A new patient said, "I heard you guys are witch doctors!"
I replied, "That depends on *which doctor* you see."

Patient: When I sneeze, every part of my body hurts.

Me: Sounds like you are suffering from fibromy*allergies*.

A certain patient of mine only comes to see me when he's hit rock bottom and can hardly walk due to the excruciating pain. The last time I had seen him was two years earlier when he came crawling into my office.

After his treatment, I said, "This is the absolute worst I've ever seen you, since the last time I saw you! And I probably won't ever see you this bad again, until the next time I see you."

Patient: Before you tell me my diagnosis, I want you to know that you don't have to sugarcoat anything. Tell it to me like it is. I'm a big girl and I can handle it.

Me: Okay, I found chronic hypolordosis with osteophytic formation and anterior juxtaposition divergence of the inferior articular facets of C5 and C6 with acute radiculalgia and unilateral myofascitis. This is complicated by degeneration of the atlantodental joint and stylo-hyoideus ligamentous calcification.

Patient: Oh my God! Okay, forget the medical terminology. What's wrong with me in layman's terms?

Me: You have a couple of bones in your neck that are out of alignment.

October 16th is World Spine Day. When I shared this with one of my patients, she asked how I was going to celebrate. I replied, "I'm getting some cham*pain* at the lum*bar* and grill."

I'm thinking of opening a theme park for chiropractors. I'm going to call it Thoracic Park.

A new patient came in looking quite nervous. I asked, "Are you okay?"

He replied, "Yes. I've heard great things about you, Dr. Friedman, and I trust you with my life."

I replied, "I'm glad one of us feels that confident."

Patient: I hurt my neck doing inclines at the gym.

Me: I'm inclined to tell you to stop doing those.

Patient: I lifted a bunch of boxes playing Santa Claus for my kids, and I hurt my back!

Me: Sounds like you need the triple-K adjustment: Kris Kringle Krack!

Patient: I've heard an apple a day keeps the doctor away, but my MD says not to eat apples and just keep coming in to see him.

Me: In that case, a doctor a day keeps the apples away.

A patient came in one day and told me that her shin hurts, and I replied, "Shin happens!"

Some patients adjust easily, and some spines require a lot of force. But, on rare occasions, simply laying a patient on their side without applying any pressure causes the bone to realign. Most patients respond, "Wow! That went before you even started!"

I have a term for when this happens: *premature crackulation!*

One day a patient who had self-diagnosed himself after doing a Google search came in.

When I shared my findings with him, he said, "That's not what's wrong with me. I know what it is."

I replied, "You think you know, but my exam shows differently."

He replied, "I don't *think*, I know!"

I said, "I agree. I don't *think* you know either."

Patient: You always know the exact spot I'm hurting!

Me: Yes, I feel your pain.

Rearrange the following letters P-N-E-S-I to form the name of an important body part that is most useful when long and erect.

What's the word I'm looking for? SPINE.

My office manager took me aside and said, "Dr. Friedman, there's a patient sitting in the waiting room who thinks he's invisible. What should I tell him?"

I responded, "Tell him I can't see him today."

Patient: I'm a total mess, and I've lost hope. It feels like the whole world has!

Me: The only Hope the world has lost is Bob.

Patient: I've got a bad migraine headache!

Me: Nope, it's a *you* grain headache. Let's fix you and turn that into a *their* grain headache!

I always stress the importance of staying hydrated and drinking water because dehydration is a major cause of joint pain and muscle spasms.

One of the excuses my patients often give me for not drinking enough water is, "It doesn't have any taste, so I don't like to drink it."

My reply is, "Oxygen doesn't have any smell, but you still choose to breathe it through your nose."

Two sisters with unusual names—Koketa and Pepsita—came to see me for a consultation. They went by the nicknames Koke and Pepsi.

I walked in, introduced myself, and said, "I've looked at your complaints, and I think you should see a different doctor!"

Their jaws dropped, and Koketa said, "But you haven't even talked to us yet and you didn't do an examination!"

I said again, "I know, but I really think you should see a different doctor. I'll make a referral."

They both looked puzzled.

"To whom?" Pepsita asked.

I replied, "Dr. Pepper!"

Their laughter almost knocked them off their chairs.

Patient: I used to have the worst posture, but since coming to see you, I don't hump anymore!

Me: Sorry to hear that. Do you need a prescription for Viagra?

Patient: I need you to adjust my wrist. I was really bad this week!

Me: You were so bad, you should be *awristed*!

Patient: I joined the Y!

Me: Y.

Patient: Because you told me I needed to exercise more.

Me: Y.

Patient: Because it has a pool and exercise classes.

Me: Y.

Patient: How come you keep asking me that?

Me: Oh, it wasn't a question; it was an acknowledgment.

A patient came in, and during my examination, I discovered that one of his legs was an inch shorter than the other. I looked over at his sneakers and said, "Well, you're wearing the wrong brand of footwear."

The patient gave me a confused look, and I replied, "You wear New Balance, but until I fix your problem, you should be wearing Off Balance!"

Patient: I'm having a hard time getting used to the cervical pillow I bought from you.

Me: It can take a little getting used to.

Patient: When I wake up, it's on the floor. I must be throwing it off the bed in the middle of the night.

Me: You think that's bad? When I first started sleeping on my cervical pillow, I had a nightmare that I ate a giant marshmallow. And the next morning, my pillow was gone!

Patient: That was an amazing adjustment! I can't believe you can jump all over me like that and not hurt yourself!

Me: And I do it all without the aid of a safety net!

Looking at a poster of a giant ocean wave hanging on my office wall, a patient asked me if it was a tsunami.

"Yes, it is," I replied. "Want to know how I know this?"

She nodded, and I pointed to an area of the painting and explained, "You see this tiny little floating speckle? That's a piece of rye bread. That makes it a tsunami on rye."

I took a patient's X-rays out of the folder and put them on the view box to go over my findings.

The patient asked, "How do I look?"

I replied, "With your eyes."

An elderly woman in her late nineties named Harriet was having her treatment while her husband Chester sat in the waiting room.

A concerned patient walked up to the front desk and said, "I don't think he's breathing!"

To my office manager's total dismay, she looked into the waiting room and saw Chester sitting in the chair with his head extended back, mouth wide open, and eyes closed. She immediately walked up to him and said, "Chester, are you okay?"

He did not respond. He just sat there stagnant, head tilted back, and not breathing.

She gently pushed on his lifeless body and said louder, "Chester, are you okay?!"

Still no response.

After Harriet's treatment, I walked with her to the front desk and noticed a disturbing look on the faces of all my employees.

As Harriet was checking out, my office manager pulled me to the side and informed me, "Chester is dead. He died in our waiting room!"

Just as I was being told the news, Harriet finished, walked into the waiting room, and approached Chester's lifeless body. She made a tight fist, punched him in the arm, and screamed, "Darn it, Chester, wake the hell up! It's time to leave."

To everyone's total amazement, Chester's head abruptly jerked forward, and he replied, "Okay dear, I'm up!"

Patient: I just got over being deathly ill after eating raw salmon.

Me: Did you mix salmon with vanilla extract? If so, you probably got *salmonilla*.

A construction worker came in with super tight muscles. I had to use my knee to break up some of the spasms.

He said, "Is that your knee?"

I replied, "Yes. You were in *need* of *knee kneading!*"

After treating a new patient, he smiled and said, "I'm happy I found you. The last chiropractor I went to was so rough when adjusting my neck, if I went to see him on a Tuesday, a second later it would be Wednesday."

With a confused look, I asked him what he meant by that, and he replied, "He knocked me into tomorrow!"

DATING A CHIROPRACTOR

I HAD A GREAT TIME TONIGHT.
I WOULD LIKE TO SEE YOU AGAIN **3** TIMES PER WEEK FOR A MONTH,
AND THEN **2** TIMES A WEEK FOR EIGHT WEEKS.

CELEBRITIES ARE PATIENTS, TOO

I never believed that chiropractors could solve my
back problem, but I stand corrected.

—ROBIN WILLIAMS

DURING ONE OF HIS VISITS, Robin Williams wasn't his usual talkative self.
He pointed to his neck and mumbled, "Please fix me!"

He laid face up on the table; I found the misalignment and

proceeded to twist his neck to realign the bone. Just as I turned his head, I felt and heard a loud crunch.

Robin fell off the treatment table and began convulsing and mumbling. "I tink you bwoke my neck!" he cried. "My entire wight arm is numb!"

Oh my God, I just paralyzed Robin Williams!

Then he looked up at me with a smile and stuck out his tongue to reveal a piece of peppermint candy, which he'd bit into just as I turned his head. After the initial shock wore off, I laughed so hard that tears rolled down my legs.

"I do not trust Dr. Friedman. He is always pulling my leg!"

—JIMMIE "J.J." WALKER

Jimmie "J. J." Walker, who starred in the hit '70s sitcom *Good Times*, came in for back pain relief and was getting great results.

One day, after his treatment, he lay on the floor and crawled out into the waiting room. Shimmying across the carpet, he held his hand to his neck and shouted, "Someone help me! I walked in here just fine! Friedman beat me up, and now I can't stand!"

Everyone's horror turned to relief when he lifted his head and they realized it was Jimmie Walker.

"Just kidding!" he said, hopping to his feet. "Friedman's adjustment was SPINE-O-MITE!"

I live in a small city off the east coast of North Carolina called Wilmington. Unlike the Las Vegas motto, our saying goes, "What goes on in Wilmington is everyone's business." News travels fast in my city, something Dean Cain, the actor who played Superman on *Lois and Clark*, wasn't used to. Here's how it went down when he was shooting a show in Wilmington:

After I reviewed Dean's X-ray, I said, "This is ironic. Do you realize I'm using X-ray vision on Superman?"

Surprising me he said, "That's one I haven't heard before."

Dean didn't realize that this was just my warmup . . .

One day, a restaurant owner in town said, "You won't believe who came in today! That handsome fellow who plays Superman on TV."

"You mean Dean Cain?" I replied.

She smiled and said, "Yes, that's the guy."

"Can you tell me what he had to eat?" I asked sinisterly.

"Sure, he had a double cheeseburger, fries, and a chocolate milkshake."

When Dean came in later that evening for a back treatment, I said, with my hands on his back, "Dean, you really should eat healthier!"

"What do you mean?" he asked.

I ran my hands along his spine. "Did you have a cheeseburger, French fries, and a chocolate shake today?"

He gasped. "You can tell what I ate by feeling my spine?"

"You can't hide much from me," I replied.

A week later, a patient of mine who owns a golf driving range said, "Guess who came by today to hit some balls?"

"Was it Dean Cain?" I asked.

"Yes!" he replied.

"How many buckets did he end up getting?"

"Two."

At Dean's appointment later that day, I touched his back and asked, "Dean, were you swinging something today? Perhaps . . . a golf club? Did you hit two buckets of golf balls?"

Dean almost fell off the table. "How can you tell that from my spine?"

"You can't hide much from me," I replied.

A few days later, someone who had just come from the local baseball batting cages told me, "Dean Cain, that guy who played Superman, was at the batting range today."

So, when Dean came in for his treatment, I said, "Looks like you gave up swinging a golf club for swinging a baseball bat!"

Wide-eyed, he said, "You are freakin' scaring me, Doc!"

"You can't hide much from me. Imagine what I can tell about you from your spine that I don't even mention!"

One of the show's producers came in later for treatment and told me that Dean had said, "This Friedman is a freakin' psychic! He can put his hands on your back and not only tell if you just ate a pizza, he knows whether it was Domino's or Papa John's!"

Sometimes I bring my portable adjusting table and an electrical muscle stimulator to celebrities' hotel rooms to treat them.

One day, I went to see Harvey Keitel, who opened the door with a bad case of bedhead that made him look like Kramer from *Seinfeld*. He ran his hand through his hair and said he had just woken up.

I entered the room and put down my equipment. "I brought an electric stim, but I see you've already been electrocuted!"

"I'm here because I need Dr. Friedman to jump my bones!"

—JENNY MCCARTHY

One of my favorite celebrity patients that I've had the privilege of treating is the late, great Andy Griffith. Our relationship turned into a wonderful friendship, and he will forever be missed.

Living in North Carolina, there is no other place in the world where the name Andy Griffith is more well known. In fact, the fictitious town in his eponymous television show, *Mayberry*, was modeled after Mount Airy, North Carolina, where Andy had grown up.

Even as popular as he was, every time he would walk into my office waiting room for his scheduled appointment, he would say to my receptionist, "My name's Andy Griffith. I'm here to see Dr. Friedman. My last name is spelled G-R-I-F-F-I-T-H."

This would be like the pope introducing himself and spelling his name for the receptionist at Saint Peter's Vatican Catholic Church.

The movie *Bruno* was being filmed on location downtown in a historic home. I brought my portable table to treat Oscar-winning actress Shirley MacLaine on set. It was a small house, and with the cast and crew, sound, lighting, and video equipment, there was no place for me to set up my treatment table.

Louis, the owner of the house, told me I could set up my table in the bathroom, which would also allow some privacy as well. So, I set up my portable adjustment table, which fit inside the bathroom with no room to spare. I couldn't bring the stool I normally sit on when doing the adjustment, so I used the toilet seat instead.

Shirley came in and lay on her back. I sat on the toilet with her head between my knees and started to work on Shirley's neck.

One of the crew members came walking into the bathroom and saw me sitting on the toilet, rubbing Shirley MacLaine's neck.

Thinking I was taking a crap, his jaw dropped in total disbelief and he quickly exited the bathroom, muttering under his breath, "I don't even wanna know! To each his own."

Shirley and I couldn't stop laughing. It's not the number-one strangest thing I've experienced while on a movie set, but it definitely comes in at *number two*.

I was called back to the set of *Bruno* after Shirley was unable to move without excruciating middle back pain, which hurt every time she would take a breath.

"I found your problem. You have a rib that is out of place."

She scoffed at me and replied, "No, I don't! I know exactly why I'm hurting. I was stabbed in that same location in a previous life and occasionally that knife wound presents itself in my current body.

When I go back to LA, I'll have some regressive hypnotherapy done and deal with it then."

"Shirley, having a rib misalignment is actually my second diagnosis. Being stabbed in a former life is my first diagnosis."

She smiled and said, "Really? You picked up on that too?"

She didn't realize I was just joking. She said to give her a full adjustment since I was there anyway, and it couldn't hurt.

Afterward, she said, "Oh my, the pain is gone. Maybe it was my rib after all."

"Applying barbecue sauce isn't the only way to fix ribs in North Carolina," I replied.

Another movie that was filmed in Wilmington is *Shadrach*, starring Andie MacDowell. She was on location filming at Orton Plantation, located in the woods right next to the Cape Fear River. It was in the heart of the summer, and the forest was infested with mosquitoes.

I carried my portable table and set it up inside Andie's trailer. Effortlessly demure, Andie entered with toilet paper dangling from one of her shoes.

Should I tell her?

I just didn't have the courage to tell her something so embarrassing. After her treatment, as I packed up, one of the co-stars walked past me. There it was again, toilet paper stuck to the back of one of his shoes.

I found my set medic friend and whispered, "I couldn't help but notice Andie and another one of the actors both have toilet paper dangling from their shoes. I guess no one has the guts to tell them?"

"That's not toilet paper!" she laughed. "Those are Bounce dryer sheets. They are a great repellant against mosquitoes!"

I went home and applied calamine lotion wishing I had known this helpful tidbit earlier.

The movie *Black Dog*, starring Patrick Swayze, Randy Travis, and Meat Loaf, was filmed in my city. When Beverly, one of my regular patients, walked into the waiting room and saw Patrick Swayze sitting there, she made a beeline for the bathroom.

When she came back, my office manager asked if everything was okay.

Beverly replied, "If I'm going to sit in the same room with Patrick Swayze, I had to put makeup on. I couldn't let him see me like that."

I was fitting Golden Globe– and Academy Award–winning actor James Earl Jones for foot orthotics. His feet are a size 14, so I had to use two full-size casting kits.

"You know what they say about a tall black man who has really big feet?" James said in his signature baritone voice.

I was too embarrassed to reply, knowing where this typical joke was heading.

James laughed at my discomfort and answered, "They wear big shoes."

Actress Lisa Hartman Black, who was staying at the Hilton, asked her assistant to make an appointment with me for a house call.

"Lisa also wants Dr. Friedman to try her pillow," the actress's assistant told my office manager.

I arrived at Lisa's hotel room a bit befuddled. Lisa showed me a rare pillow she had purchased overseas that was filled with native organic husk. She asked me to lie on it and give her my professional opinion if it was good for her neck.

So, I lay on the bed and tried out the pillow. I fell in love with it! In fact, it was the most comfortable pillow I had ever put my head on!

When Lisa's movie shoot ended, her assistant stopped by my office and handed the pillow to my office manager, and said with gratitude, "Lisa was so happy with Dr. Friedman's magic touch at her hotel room, she wants him to have her pillow as a token of her appreciation."

My employees' minds went somewhere else . . .

One of the most memorable films I have worked on was Brandon Lee's *The Crow*. Lucky me, I got to treat the entire cast and crew. In this movie, a bunch of greasy gang members vandalize and burn down parts of the city on Halloween night.

David Patrick Kelly (T-Bird), Angel David (Skank), and Laurence Mason (Tin Tin) all visited my office during their lunch break dressed in their gang member costumes. The three men took seats in my waiting room.

One waiting patient shivered in her seat, clenching her purse with both hands. The others looked wary, too. Another patient preferred to wait outside in his car until he was ready to be seen. When another patient walked in and saw the "hoodlums," he said, "I don't want no trouble. I have three kids and a pregnant wife at home!"

David Patrick Kelly laughingly announced to the group that they were from the set of *The Crow* and were just in costume.

Sighs of relief and requests for autographs followed. The patient who said he would wait outside for his appointment had driven off and missed all the excitement.

Another celebrity I've been honored to work with is John Travolta. He's even flown me to his house in Florida to treat him and his family, and while I was there, we got to spend some time getting to know each other. I'm happy to be able to call him my friend.

John is truly one of the most down-to-earth, unpretentious celebs I've ever met. He is always happy to sign an autograph, and at restaurants, he quite often goes into the kitchen after a meal to personally thank the chef. How many people do you know that will do that?

One day, we were at a restaurant called Alleigh's, which had a giant game room, bar, and karaoke club.

Someone in John's entourage said, "JT, you should go up and sing."

In a blink, John was on stage singing one of his hit songs from *Grease*.

A guy at the bar shouted, "Damn, he sounds just like the real guy! He even looks like him!"

One day Travolta invited me to see the Brad Pitt movie *Troy*. When the movie ended, we exited the theater and John said, "Be right back!" as he opened the door to the projection room and walked up the stairs. I heard someone scream, "HOLY SHIT!" and a minute later John came back down the stairs. I asked him what was that all about and he told me, "I just wanted to thank the projectionist for the great job he's doing up there. His role is just as important as the director of the films we star in. Without him, no one could see the movies we make."

I replied, "I hope he brought a change of underwear. I think what he shouted out loud actually took place."

My patient, Vince, told me he saw John Travolta coming out of the shower at the YMCA just as he was walking in. He had stopped, looked at John, and said, "Hi, John! It looks like we have something in common."

Travolta scoured Vince's naked body, glanced at his own, and replied, "Um, I don't think so."

"Yes, we do," Vince insisted. "We are both Dr. David Friedman's patients."

I got called to the set of *Black Knight*, starring Martin Lawrence. Gil Junger, the director of the movie, was in severe pain.

"Paula Abdul is our choreographer and I tried to dance with her. I immediately felt something in my back pop," Gil told me.

Shaking my head, I said, "No wonder you're in pain! Trying to dance with one of the most well-known choreographers in the world is like a rookie boxer sparring with Mike Tyson!"

Val Kilmer, star of *Batman*, *Top Gun*, and *Tombstone*, lay on the table. My therapist placed electrodes on his back and told him, "I'm going to turn up the machine now. You will feel your muscles slowly start to jump. You don't want to take it too strong, so let me know when it's at a comfortable level."

Just as she started to turn the machine to the lowest setting, Val's entire body began to shake aggressively. Kilmer shouted, "Oh my God! Turn it down! Turn it down!"

My therapist quickly turned the machine off. "I'm so sorry. I only turned it up to five and most people take it to around fifty," she cried.

He gave her his charming smile. "Just kidding."

I treated the cast and crew for the popular hit series *Dawson's Creek*. One day, I received an emergency call that someone had been seriously injured and production had come to a halt.

When I arrived on the set, executive producer Greg Prange met me in the parking lot and told me that one of the leads, Michelle Williams, was in such severe pain that she could hardly breathe.

I carried my portable treatment table into a room where I saw Michelle Williams lying on the floor curled up, crying in agony.

I asked her what the cause of her pain was, and she whimpered, "Don . . . (sniffle) . . . Don . . . (deep breath) . . . Donny Osmond hugged me."

I looked at Greg and said, "Did she just say Donny Osmond hugged her?"

He nodded. "Donny is doing a cameo on set today and gave Michelle a big hello hug, and she heard a loud pop in her back and couldn't breathe."

"Darn it!" I said to Michelle. "This makes the third time I had to help someone out who was injured by a Donny Osmond hug!"

She laughed, and I proceeded to fix the Osmond-induced back injury.

I worked on critically acclaimed actor Dennis Hopper while he was filming the movie *Super Mario Brothers*. After having great relief from his back pain from my treatments, he made a weekly scheduled appointment to come see me.

"It's been a rough week, and I need some major back popping," Dennis announced one afternoon.

I replied, "You've come to the right place. I am the Dennis Hopper popper!"

I adjusted Woody Harrelson while he was filming a movie in North Carolina. I asked him for a signed headshot, but he didn't have any with him. He said he would sign one for me and give it to Beth, the set medic.

After the movie ended, I had seen Beth a few times, but she had forgotten to bring me the signed picture of Woody. One day while on the set for another film, I said to Beth, "Don't forget about my Woody."

"Oh, don't you worry about that Dr. Friedman," Beth assured me as she held up her clenched fist. "I'm holding on real tight to your Woody!"

All around us, jaws dropped.

I performed a dynamometer grip strength analysis on Lindsay Wagner, who starred in the hit TV series *The Bionic Woman*.

After she squeezed the device to test her strength, I looked at the results with disappointment. "With you being the bionic woman and all, I really expected you'd have much more power than that. Let's have you try it one more time."

This time, as she squeezed the strength-testing device, I mimicked the high-pitched sounds from the series whenever the character lifted something heavy.

I looked at the result of her second attempt and said, "Much better! I knew the sound effects were what made you so strong."

As part of the excitement of treating so many gracious, fun celebrities, I frame and hang their autographed headshots on my office walls. Not only does this serve as a Hall of Fame–type display, but it also showcases celebrities that rely on chiropractic care.

Pat Hingle's glossy photo keeps company with the likes of Alec Baldwin, Paul Newman, John Travolta, and Diane Lane, to name just a few. Pat stands out as one of the few character actors I've treated (along with the hoodlum guys from *The Crow*).

While Pat is best known for his small role as Commissioner Gordon in *Batman*, millions have enjoyed watching him in his many roles and cameos on *Cheers*, *Matlock*, *Murder, She Wrote*, *Magnum P.I.*, and others.

One day, a new patient was admiring my wall and exclaimed, "OH MY GOD! No way! You worked on Pat Hingle?! He is my *favorite* actor of all time. I've seen everything he's been in. Can I shake the hand of the chiropractor who has had his hands on the back of the amazing Pat Hingle?!"

As much of a fan I personally am of Pat, I was taken aback that, of all the A-listers on my wall, this patient was star-struck for Pat.

The next time I saw Pat, I told him about my new patient's reaction. Pat laughed. "That totally made my day! Next time that patient comes in, let me know."

That is exactly what I did. Pat made time to surprise my patient, who was so exhilarated that you would've thought Elvis Presley had entered the building.

A new patient hobbled down the hallway of my office, awkwardly lifting one leg and dropping the other.

The occupation on his chart said, "A Walk to Remember," and all I could think was, *you got that right.*

Puzzled, I inquired further and learned that the patient had triggered his sciatica after working on Nicholas Sparks's movie *A Walk to Remember.*

Legendary kickboxing and karate expert Jean-Claude Van Damme was filming *Cyborg.* I had a hunch that he wasn't all he was cracked up to be, and I told him so: "People believe you're this big, bad tough karate guy, but if you and I were in a fight, I could totally kick your ass with both arms and legs tied behind *your back.*"

Meat Loaf was in town filming the Patrick Swayze movie *Black Dog,* and

I received a message that he wanted to come in after-hours for treatment. I told my office manager, "I'll be staying late today for Meat Loaf."

She scratched her head and replied, "Here at the clinic?"

I said, "Yes. It will be around seven o'clock, right after we close."

She said, "You being such a health nut, I didn't think you were a fan!"

I told her, "Yes, I grew up in the 80s, and Meat Loaf was a big part of that decade."

My office manager replied, "What's so great about plain old meatloaf?"

I responded, "Let me sleep on it. I'll give you an answer in the morning."

She said, "You can't tell me now?"

I replied, "Also, 'Two Out of Three Ain't Bad.'"

With a look of total confusion, she put her hand in the air. "Just forget I asked. I hope you enjoy your dinner!" she said and walked away.

Back in the nineties, I was on the set of the motion picture *Virus*, starring Jamie Lee Curtis, Donald Sutherland, and William Baldwin. One day, Baldwin was face down on my table when Jamie Lee Curtis quietly walked up behind him, grabbed his butt cheeks, and gave them a good squeeze.

Thinking it was me, Baldwin put up his fist and shouted, "What the hell are you doing Friedman?!"

We had a good laugh once he figured out that I wasn't the culprit.

JUST A LITTLE MISUNDERSTANDING

SOMETIMES IN MY CLINIC, words can be misinterpreted. This can happen when a patient is lying on their stomach with their mouth muffled by face paper. However, it also occurs when a patient and I are talking face-to-face. Being from up north, it's sometimes my inability to speak "southern." Other times, it's because certain gestures and words can have several different meanings. Here are a few misunderstandings that have brought some chuckles over the years.

My patient pointed to her wedding ring and said, "I've had enough! I can't get rid of this son of a bitch, and I wake up miserable every day! What do you recommend?"

"Have you two tried seeing a counselor?" I asked. "If you can't work it out, I can recommend a good divorce attorney."

Her jaw dropped, and she exclaimed, "I'm talking about this swollen knuckle! I need to do something about this arthritis."

"Are you taking the rest of the day off?" I asked a patient to make small talk before beginning her treatment.

"Why? What are you planning to do to me?" she asked, alarmed. "Will I have to go home and lie on an ice pack the rest of the day?"

"Hey, it's my W-T-F guy!" I said as the patient walked in.

He looked confused and said, "Why are you calling me a What-the-f*ck guy?!"

"What?" I said. "No! You come to see me on **W**ednesdays, **T**uesdays, and **F**ridays!"

Me: I'm just waiting on your X-ray.

Female: But I've never dated anyone named Ray.

A woman was lying face down on the treatment table, moving her hands back and forth, trying to get comfortable.

"Is something wrong?" I asked.

"Yes," she replied. "Where do I put these things?"

"Just drop them to the floor," I instructed.

She looked at me aghast. "Drop my boobs to the floor?!"

During a neck adjustment of a very tense patient, I instructed him to try to relax. "Maybe do some visualization. Try thinking of the beach."

But his muscles only became tighter.

"What happened?" I asked.

"You told me to think of my wife."

"No," I stammered. "I said think of the BEACH."

"Can chiropractic help sinus problems?" my patient asked.

"Yes," I said. "According to *Gray's Anatomy*, a misalignment of the second cervical vertebra can affect the sinuses."

With a confused look, she replied, "Really? I must have missed that episode. I thought I'd watched them all."

Anita and her husband had been trying for eight years to conceive a child. Her fertility expert had tried several things to no avail.

I discovered from her X-ray that Anita's third lumbar vertebra was misaligned, and I shared with her how the nerve from this bone supplies nerve flow to her uterus. Eight weeks after correcting her low back, Anita was pregnant!

Her manager at the department store where Anita worked told me, "Doc, you may want to talk to Anita. She's going around the store shouting, 'My chiropractor got me pregnant!'"

I couldn't help but notice how much a new patient of mine looked like a girl I knew in high school. "You look like Helen Brown," I said.

She gave me a nasty look and replied, "You don't look so great in blue yourself!"

It was December 1999, three days before the dreaded "Y2K," when it was predicted all the computers would stop working. The media warned that it could be the end of times. Most everyone stocked up on food, water, and money—including me!

I was chatting with a patient after her treatment, and I asked, "So do you have your Y2K stuff ready for this weekend?"

She gave me the angriest look I've ever seen and exclaimed, "Why in the heck do you think I need that stuff—because I'm over 50 years old?!" With that, she stormed out of the office.

I couldn't understand why she got so angry. In fact, it's all I could think about the entire afternoon. I replayed our conversation over and over in my mind. Then it hit me! She must have thought I said, "KY stuff."

I imagined her conversation with her husband when she got home: "That damn Dr. Friedman asked me if I had my KY stuff ready for this weekend! The nerve! What a perv!"

My assistant led a patient to the treatment room and said, "Dr. Friedman will be with you shortly."

When I came in, he asked, "Why do you let your employees make fun of people's height?"

"I'm not sure what you mean," I admitted.

"Your assistant called me shorty."

Patient: I have several fatty bumps on my back. Should I be worried about them?

Me: No, they are called lipomas. They're *benign*.

Patient: What? Please count again. I thought there would only *be three*.

A patient told me that when she went to the pharmacy to pick up a prescription, the pharmacist asked for her date of birth. She shared how excited she was to know he would be sending her a birthday gift.

A patient asked me for a recommendation for something natural to help his anxiety, and I told him to get skullcap, which is an herbal product that's often used for anxiety. The following week he returned wearing a yarmulke.

"The pain is on your left side?" I asked a patient with a bad back, as I examined that part of his back.

"Right," he replied.

I switched to the right side and started examining.

"Why did you switch sides?" he asked.

"You said the pain is on your right side," I replied.

Laughing, the patient said, "*Right*, meaning you were already on the correct side."

Patient: I just had an MRI done, and I have some information.

Me: Great, what did they find?

Patient: I have some information.

Me: Yes, I'm glad you do.

Patient: Huh? You're *glad* I have information?

Me: Yes. What did they tell you?

Patient: Once again, they told me I have *information*!
  (It was then that I realized she was saying *inflammation*.)

A patient told me she had carpal tunnel syndrome and asked me if I treated wrists.

"Yes, I do. Which one is bothering you?" I replied.

She answered, "Both of them hurt."

So, I wrote on her chart and said out loud, "Wrist pain, *bilateral.*"

Her jaw dropped and she exclaimed, "No I'm not! I prefer men."

Born and bred in North Carolina, Glen asked, "Dr. Friedman, you're into all this healthy eating stuff and nutrition. My wife tells me I don't eat healthy, and I reckon I could use your help. Do you have any suggestions?"

"For starters, you should add fish to your diet," I suggested.

"I eat crappy every week," he said.

"Yes, you do, and that's why you need to add fish to your diet. They offer healthy omega-fatty acids, which are great for the brain and heart."

"Doc, I eat crappy!"

"I understand that, which is why you should add fish to your diet."

"Then why can't I eat crappy?"

Frustrated, I emphatically answered, "Because you need to eat healthily."

"And what should I do?"

"Start by eating fish."

"But I eat crappy!" Glen was turning red. "How can that not be good for me?"

I said, "Because eating crappy is not good for you!"

Glen then said, "But you said I need to eat fish."

"Yes, you do."

"I'm a crappy eater!"

"Yes, Glen, I know. I get that! That's why you need to add fish to your diet!"

(As I would eventually discover, crappy is a popular breed of fish in the South. I now advocate strongly for eating a crappy diet. But brush your teeth afterward; otherwise, you'll have crappy breath.)

Hank came in with excruciating back pain. "Dr. Friedman, I did something I shouldn't have. My wife is out of town, and I hope she doesn't find out!"

"What did you do?" I asked.

"I got into a little trouble messing with a backhoe."

My mouth dropped. "Hank," I said. "You're a married man. What are you doing messing around with a . . ." I could hardly get the word out. "*Ho?*"

"I know. I know," he replied. "I shouldn't have. But with the wife being out of town, I guess I went a little crazy."

"Well, considering you can hardly move, I guess you learned your lesson."

"Yeah, my wife told me to limit riding her to just an hour, but I went for four hours!"

Again, I could barely get the words out. "Hank, are you telling me your wife knows about and approves of your indiscretions?"

He laughed and said, "Of course, she approves. She helped me pick her out!"

Being a city boy, I would later learn that a backhoe is a type of excavating equipment used on farms.

I sell a supplement in my office for sinus relief called Phytophed (*phyto* means plant).

After recommending it to one of my patients, she told my front desk attendee, "Dr. Friedman wants me to get what he feeds his dog Fido."

Looking at her strangely, the attendee said, "He doesn't have a dog."

"You know, the Fido Fed stuff Doc recommends for sinuses."

Patient: I fell and hurt my shoulder. Whatcha think it is, Doc?

Me: Dislocation.

Patient: I'm so glad I'm in the right place. I knew you would figure it out. What seems to be wrong with my shoulder?

Me: Dislocation.

Patient: Yes, I came to *this location* because a friend of mine said you could help. What do you think is wrong with my shoulder?

While I was checking Paul's back, I asked if he experienced any indigestion.

He replied, "Yes, I get it all the time. I eat TUMS like candy. How did you know?"

I said, "Because your sixth thoracic vertebra is misaligned and the nerve that exits that segment innervates the stomach."

I adjusted his T6, and he got up from the treatment table in total shock. "Oh my God! My indigestion is gone! I had no idea you could help that."

He continued to see me for an adjustment to his T6 and experienced great relief from his chronic indigestion.

One day, Paul was at work and saw a coworker chewing TUMS. He asked the coworker if he suffered from indigestion, and the coworker replied that he suffers from severe heartburn and rarely can go a single day without indigestion.

Paul told him, "Man, you have got to go see my chiropractor! He specializes in fixing indigestion."

Paul's coworker came in to see me, and after his third adjustment, he was definitely seeing a reduction in his indigestion.

One day he called to cancel his appointment because he had to take care of his wife, who had hurt her back. My receptionist asked, "Why don't you have your wife come in and see Dr. Friedman?"

"Why would I do that?" he asked. "Paul told me Dr. Friedman specializes in fixing indigestion. What does he know about treating back pain?"

I was walking down the hall with a patient named Barbara, and she was telling me that her body hurts at night when she sleeps.

"How do you sleep?" I asked.

"Oh, I'm totally wild in the sack!" she replied, just as a male patient was walking past us.

This patient did a double take, put his thumb to his ear and pinky to his lips, and mouthed, "Have her call me!"

We sell a moist heat wrap called the *bed buddy*. It's filled with rice, and you put it in the microwave for a couple of minutes. I recommended this to a patient.

That evening, the woman's angry husband called my office and demanded to speak to me. My office manager told him I was busy seeing patients and asked if there was anything she could do to help him.

He replied, "My wife came in today, and when I asked how her appointment went, she told me after looking at her X-ray, Dr. Friedman told her she needed a new bed buddy! Is this accurate?"

My office manager told him to hold on while she pulled her chart. When she came back, she replied, "Yes, I'm looking at your wife's chart now, and it clearly says that Dr. Friedman did recommend that your wife get a new bed buddy."

(His wife eventually told him that the *bed buddy* was a heating pad.)

One day, while I was in the middle of treating an older couple, my assistant walked into the room and said, "There's a patient on the phone. He wants to know—when he's done using his bed buddy each night, should he sleep with it?"

I replied, "Tell him to use the bed buddy for an hour and when he's done, just toss it on the floor."

The couple almost fainted.

John asked, "Why am I getting such bad headaches?"

I replied, "It's from pressure at the base of the skull called the occiput."

When John got home, his wife asked him, "What did the doctor say is causing your headaches?"

He responded, "Doc said it's coming from my octopus. I guess I have to go see him eight times before it's fixed."

A patient came in one day with pain along his hip. After his exam, I told him that his iliac crest had fallen out.

He replied, "Crest?! Did I get toothpaste on my shirt?"

A bone out of alignment is called a "subluxation." One day, I was sharing my report of findings with a patient, and I showed her how a subluxation in her spine was the reason for her pain and explained that I was going to remove it.

Later that day, her husband called the office and said, "I just spoke to my wife about Dr. Friedman's findings. She said he found a submarine in her spine that needs to be removed?"

I always review patients' activities of daily living with them so that their adjustments hold. I cover everything from sitting and sleeping to driving habits and proper posture. One day, I was treating a patient who sat at a computer all day, which was contributing to her neck and back pain.

"Your biggest problem is sitting," I told her. "You sit too much."

She replied, "No, just once a day."

I responded, "Yes, but then you sit for eight hours."

She laughed and said, "No, but that did happen once after I ate some really bad Mexican food."

(She'd apparently thought I said, "Your biggest problem is that you *shit* too much"!)

I do a move called "axial traction" on the neck. I grab the base of the skull and quickly pull it to decompress the spine. The move is very *uplifting*.

One day, after performing this technique on a patient, I told her, "You may have felt that way low," and I pointed to her low back.

She asked, "Did you just say my butt's as big as J. Lo?"

Patient: I won't be able to come in for a few weeks because I'm having surgery on my legs.

Me: Why are you having surgery?

Patient: Because my veins are too close together.

Me: I've never heard of such a thing.

Patient: Well, that's what the doctor told me. I have very close veins.

Me: Oh. You have *varicose veins*.

I walked in and saw a patient reading a book. I said, "Oh, I see you are into violins."

He seemed appalled by my comment and said, "I am not a *violent* person!"

"If you're not a violin person, why read about the topic?" I asked.

He said, "*This* is a book about the history of musical instruments used in the symphony."

After reexamining a patient, I told her that she was now in the number-two phase, and she asked, "Did you just call me two-faced?"

A patient said, "Please explain what you are going to do before you do it so I can share everything with my husband later."

I replied, "Okay. The first thing I'm going to do is a maneuver on your neck."

She looked at me strangely and said, "You are going to put manure on my neck?!"

I treated a patient named Gary when he was fifteen years old. A decade later, he came back in for treatment.

"You definitely grew some!" I noted.

Gary said, "Did you just tell me I am definitely gruesome?"

"Dr. Friedman," a patient exclaimed, "I hurt my back yesterday from a fall. I slipped and fell on my niece!"

I replied, "That's terrible! Is she okay?"

She looked at me glazed in confusion and responded, "Is who okay?"

I said, "Your niece. You said you fell on her!"

"No," she said, "I fell on my *knees!*"

A patient said, "My back seems to be feeling better since I got these amputee shoes."

I replied, "Amputee?"

She said, "Yes, and I got a really good deal on them."

Still confused, I said, "I guess you would . . . because the amputees didn't need them?"

She laughed out loud and said, "I didn't say *amputee*, I said *M-B-T*."

(Turns out, MBT—Masai Barefoot Technology—is a popular brand of shoes.)

I have a patient who dyes her hair different colors—purple, yellow, pink—that are very bright and fluorescent. During one of her visits, she came to see me with severe back pain.

"What caused your back to hurt?" I asked.

"Well, I got a new job, and all the stairs are really starting to bother me."

I thought about that for a moment and suggested, "Maybe you wouldn't have to deal with so many stares if your hair wasn't so attention-grabbing."

She gave me an angry look and said, "As in *staircase*. I have to climb a lot of *stairs*, not stares!"

A woman was lying face down on the table and while talking to me through the face paper, she told me that her Netflix had just disconnected.

I said, "That's too bad, they have some great binge-worthy programs."

"Binge-worthy?" she asked, turning her head to the side. "I just told you my *necklace* disconnected."

A man came in who was referred to my office by one of my patients, Kay. The first thing he said to me was "F-U-C-K . . ." and I was completely taken aback. It wasn't until he completed his sentence, ". . . tell her I said hello!" that I realized he had said, "If you see Kay."

A woman brought her husband in to see me. I asked what was bothering him, and she cut in and said, "My husband is limping and stupid!"

I said, "Stupid?"

She replied, "No, I said stooping."

"Dr. Friedman, there's a really bad giraffe in the waiting room!" a patient exclaimed.

I replied, "A giraffe?"

She said, "Yes! It comes in from the front door every time someone opens it, and that damn giraffe makes me wish I'd brought a jacket!"

It took me a few minutes to realize that she was saying "a bad draft."

Patient: I've been pruning a lot, and now it hurts my back when I sit.

Me: You shouldn't eat a lot of prunes because they *can* cause excessive stools.

Patient: What? No. I said SIT! I've been pruning my bushes in a sitting position, and it hurts my back!

Patient: I was lifting something and felt my back jerk.

Me: Did you just call me a jerk?!

Patient: I had a big cramp this morning.

Me: That's awesome! A healthy gut is a healthy body.

Patient: I said *cramp*, not *crap*!

Patient: Dr. Friedman, who is that playing on the radio?

Me: Yes.

Patient: Who?

Me: No, not The Who. Yes!

Patient: Not who yes, huh? Are you going to tell me, or do I need to guess who?

Me: No, it's not The Guess Who either. How many times do I need to tell you?

Patient: I'm not following. I just want to know *who* is singing the song playing right now.

Me: And I've already said, WHO is not singing the song playing right now!

Patient: Are you going to tell me or not?

Me: YES!

Patient: Okay, then tell me.

Me: YES!

Patient: Is this a trick?

Me: Cheap Trick? No, it's not them.

Patient: I know it's not Cheap Trick, darn it! WHO is it?!

Me: I already told you, it's not the WHO, it's YES!
(Patient shakes his head and lies on the treatment table.)

Patient: Fine then, don't tell me.

A patient of mine had carpal tunnel syndrome. I recommended that she take vitamin B6 for the wrist pain. The next time she came in, I asked her if she'd gotten the B6.

"I didn't have to get it," she said. "I already had some B12 at home, so I just cut the tablets in half."

(Well, at least she's good at math!)

After opening my clinic, I purchased a three-foot cement plant stand with a large gold vase and a beautiful faux floral arrangement. A patient named Pauline told me to let her know if I ever decided to get rid of it because she absolutely loved it.

As the years went by, I decided to give the office a much-needed modern makeover, and the giant floral arrangement no longer went with the new office decor.

When Pauline came in for a maintenance visit, I told her she could have the stand, vase, and floral arrangement that she had been admiring for so long. She was happy to hear the news. I figured she'd come back another day with someone to help her carry it out to her car. I said goodbye and went to see my next patient.

Meanwhile, Pauline picked up the cement stand and its adornment and slowly walked down the hall, past my front desk person, and into the waiting room. Another patient politely held the door for her and proceeded to help Pauline put everything in her car.

My office manager's jaw dropped, and she ran out to the parking lot to confront this *thief* walking out with our property. After discovering that I had given the stand and vase to Pauline, she apologized and laughed.

As a health expert for Lifetime Television's morning show, I was flying to Florida and New York one week every month. So, I hired an associate doctor to see my patients when I went out of town.

When I returned, many of my patients told me, "You sure hired an affectionate doctor to fill in for you. After the adjustment, he gave me a big hug."

I was puzzled by this, and after the third patient told me the same thing, I decided to ask my associate doctor about it.

Before I could ask, he said, "Dr. Friedman, your patients seem to really love you. Many of them asked me for a big hug after their treatment."

Now I was really confused. "I don't hug my patients," I told him. "What gave you that idea?"

He replied, "Some of them hold both of their hands out and wiggle them, asking for a hug."

I couldn't stop laughing! I broke the news to him: "They weren't asking you for a hug. Those are the patients I'm treating for carpal tunnel syndrome. They were holding out both arms and wiggling their wrists to remind you to check their hands."

A woman came in suffering from chronic headaches. During the consultation, I asked if she ground her teeth, and she confirmed that she did. I told her that it's common for teeth grinding to cause a misalignment of the temporomandibular joint (TMJ), which can cause a headache that radiates to the side of the head and face.

The next day she came back for her first treatment. After I adjusted her spine and neck, she got up from the table to leave. I saw my note on her chart that I was supposed to check her jaw, and I said to her, "Oh, one more thing we forgot," and I pointed to my cheek.

She leaned over and gave me a big kiss on my cheek.

After I told her I was referring to a jaw adjustment, she was so embarrassed. I tried to put her at ease by saying, "That's okay, I didn't get my recommended daily allowance of cheek kisses today."

A patient asked me, "On the days I can't come in because I have to work, is there anything you recommend that I take for the pain?"

I told her, "Take Aleve."

She ended up not going to work for a week. She thought I said, "Take *a leave* of absence."

A woman came in to have her regular back discomfort treated, and she told me she had scheduled an appointment to see an orthopedic doctor to fix her finger. I asked what had happened, and she told me she had jammed her middle finger playing volleyball, and it was so swollen that she couldn't extend it. I let her know that I treat extremities and would be happy to look at it for her.

She replied, "I thought chiropractors only treat backs."

I schooled her and then examined her jammed middle finger. I told her to totally relax her hand, and I snapped the finger back into place. She was absolutely awestruck at the total relief of pain and increased mobility. She told me she was canceling her appointment to see the orthopedist.

When she went to my waiting room, she held up her middle finger (aka "shooting the bird") and shouted to the group of people, "Look at this! All because of Friedman! Can you believe it?!"

Everyone just sat there in shock. Then she exclaimed, "Dr. Friedman is a magician. I had no idea he could fix fingers!"

The waiting room let out a collective sigh of relief.

I wish I had a photo of her with her middle finger in the air. My caption on social media would have been, "Another happy patient at Friedman Chiropractic."

Patient: My neighbor referred me and said you really know your stuff.

Me: I've been doing this for over thirty years. It's just trial and error.

Patient: WHAT?! You were put on trial for an error. Did the patient die?

On his initial paperwork, a patient wrote, "I experience severe sphe-nopalatine ganglioneuralgia, and the last episode almost killed me!"

While I consider myself relatively smart (after all, I did author a neuroanatomy textbook), I had never heard of this life-threatening disease—or I was completely drawing a blank.

I tried to look it up in *The Merck Manual*, a medical reference book that lists all the serious health conditions and diseases. It was not there. So, I did a Google search, and I found it: sphenopalatine ganglioneuralgia is the medical term for an "ice cream headache" or "brain freeze."

I'm not making that up. It's a cold, hard fact.

One time a lady wrote on her intake paperwork, "My psychotic nerve is bothering me."

As I began questioning her about her mental health, I quickly realized she meant "sciatic nerve."

Me: You're having some serious gut issues, and we need to take a GI series.

Patient: But I've never served in the military.

Me: What does that have to do with anything?

Patient: You said I need a GI series.

Me: GI means gastrointestinal.

A ninety-year-old patient came in one day. Her spinal adjustment went well, and I told her, "You achieved some great movement!"

While escorting her back to the waiting room, she turned the other way and said, "Then I guess I should go into the bathroom."

(I learned that day to never tell an elderly patient they achieved some great movement.)

Back when my practice first opened, I took out a huge front-page newspaper advertisement, introducing myself to the community. The ad started with "Looking for a new doctor? Meet Dr. David Friedman."

At the time, there were only a handful of chiropractors in my small city. Unfortunately, two days before my ad was set to publish, a local chiropractor who was loved by all unexpectedly died of a heart attack.

When people read my advertisement, they thought I was implying, "Looking for a new doctor (now that yours is dead)? Meet Dr. David Friedman."

Needless to say, I didn't start out my career with much love from my community. I also learned that it's not easy to get egg off the side of a building.

Patient: I went to see a chiropractor about a week back, and he told me I have tendinitis in my elbow.

Me: What does your elbow have to do with a weak back?

Patient: My back is fine!

Me: But you just told me you saw a chiropractor about a weak back.

"I'm calling to make an appointment for my wife," the person on the other line told my receptionist. "She's pregnant and having a lot of back pain."

"Is this her first child?" my receptionist asked, to which the caller replied, "No, this is her husband!"

My new patient intake form asks, "Closest relative?" and a patient wrote, "Half a mile away."

One of my patients heard that I occasionally treat dogs and asked if she could bring her puppy, Fifi, in for treatment because he was having hip issues. I told her I'd be happy to see little Fifi. The next morning, I walked into the exam room, only to discover that Fifi was a 195-pound Great Dane!

I exclaimed, "Great dane in the morning! Are you sure this isn't your pet horse?"

A patient was reading a pamphlet on how chiropractic can help with temporomandibular joint (TMJ) dysfunction, which is a pain in the area of the jawbones.

She said, "I had no idea you could do jaws!"

"I'm actually pretty good at it," I said and hummed the *Jaws* movie theme: *duuuunnnn duun . . . duuunnnnnnnn dun dun dun dun dun dun dun dun dun dun dunnnnnnnnnnn dunnnn.*

"No, I mean do you adjust people's jawbones?" she asked, straight-faced.

(Not everyone gets my humor.)

Patient: I have been experiencing vertigo and ringing in my ears. Sometimes this makes me nauseated, and I lose my balance. What do you think it is?

Me: Ménière's.

Patient: "No, Dr. Friedman, not YOUR EARS—I'm talking about mine!"

(Ménière's disease—pronounced, "mine ears"—is the name of an inner ear disorder.)

A patient slipped on the deck of his new boat while cleaning it and was having excruciating rib pain. "I came right over," he said. "I think I pulled a muscle."

I examined him and confirmed this. "Yes, the intercostal." (This is the name of the muscle between the ribs he had strained.)

"Nope," he replied. "Unfortunately, I haven't had a chance to take the boat out on the intercoastal yet."

Patient: Why do I get headaches every time I drink red wine?

Me: It's the nitrates.

Patient: So, if I pay the day rates, that won't happen?

Years back, I took out a large ad in the yellow pages. In bold letters under my name, the ad read "If after evaluating your condition, I feel that I can help you, I'll refer you to another physician."

The person doing this ad had made a typo and left off the "'t." It was supposed to read, "If after evaluating your condition, I feel I CAN'T help you, I'll refer you to another physician."

I didn't get many calls from that ad.

The walls between treatment rooms are very thin, and sometimes a patient in one room can hear what another is saying. While I take precautions against this for my patients' privacy by playing music, sometimes it doesn't drown out everything.

For instance: I was speaking with a patient in room A, and she said, "I'm so excited. I finally got my vibrator. But I'm not sure I'm using it right. Can I demonstrate for you, and you tell me if I'm going too deep?" She reached into her pocketbook and showed me her new back massager.

After her treatment, I walked into room B, where my next patient sat dumbfounded. He gave me a smile and exclaimed, "Doc, you have the absolute best job in the world!"

A woman brought in her twelve-year-old daughter, who had fallen off a trampoline and hurt her lower back.

After I adjusted the girl's spine, I used a red skin pencil (a medical marker) and drew two small Xs in the exact location I wanted the therapist to place the muscle stim pads.

After four treatments, the mother asked me, "Where can I get that healing skin pencil? I've carefully watched every time you drew the Xs, and I think I can put those magic healing red marks on her back myself."

Patient: Can you write me a note to stay out of work for the rest of the week?

Me: No, I can't do that without cause.

Patient: I do have cause. Cause I hate my job!

WEIGHTY WIT

A PATIENT WITH A LARGE BELLY TOLD ME, "I know *exactly* what's wrong with my back: it's too far away from my front."

Patient: I wish I could eat pizza, but I'm watching what I eat.

Me: So, order Domino's, and eat it in front of a mirror.

"Dr. Friedman," an obese patient said as she climbed on the table, "you can probably guess that I am into fitness."

"You are into fitness?" I asked, confused.

"Yes, *fitness* big butt into these tight jeans."

⋯⋯⋯⋯⋯⋯⋯⋯⋯⋯⋯⋯⋯⋯⋯⋯⋯⋯⋯⋯⋯⋯⋯⋯⋯⋯⋯⋯⋯

One day, a woman asked me to recommend something natural she could take to help improve her eyesight, and I told her about bilberry, which is an herb that helps with macular degeneration.

The next week she came in, and I asked her if she'd gotten the stuff I recommended for her eyes.

She replied, "No, I decided I didn't want to get fat, and I'll just deal with my eye issues."

I was puzzled by this and asked her what she meant.

She said, "You told me to get Pillsbury, and as much as I love eating their cookies, they go straight to my hips."

⋯⋯⋯⋯⋯⋯⋯⋯⋯⋯⋯⋯⋯⋯⋯⋯⋯⋯⋯⋯⋯⋯⋯⋯⋯⋯⋯⋯⋯

Patient: I'm getting married in a few months and I have to lose weight before the wedding. Any suggestions?

Me: Well, for starters, you need to eat clean.

Patient: I do. I always wash my hands before I eat anything.

⋯⋯⋯⋯⋯⋯⋯⋯⋯⋯⋯⋯⋯⋯⋯⋯⋯⋯⋯⋯⋯⋯⋯⋯⋯⋯⋯⋯⋯

A patient says, "I don't know why I'm so overweight. I eat a balanced diet! I hold an equal-sized ice cream cone in each hand."

Patient: Why can't I lose weight?

Me: Because you think *resistance training* means refusing to go to the gym.

A patient told me that, when she walks, she gets pain in her cow muscle.

"A pain where?" I asked.

She repeated, "A pain in my cow muscle."

I told her that I'd never heard of this muscle and asked her to point to the area of pain. When she pointed to her calf, I said, "Oh, you mean your calf muscle!"

"Honey," she replied, "that's not a calf anymore. Those skinny days are long gone. Now, it's a cow muscle."

Patient: I need to eat better. My weight seems to fluctuate.

Me: Yes, that could be from all the fluck you ate.

Patient: I've finally decided to do something about my weight!

Me: What?

Patient: Lie!

....

Patient: I have great news! I just lost ten pounds!

Me: If you were a drug dealer, you wouldn't be so happy about that.

....

A patient I'd been seeing for decades came in one day and said, "Your treatment tables are too narrow, and I have a hard time keeping myself from falling off. Why did you get rid of the big treatment tables you used to have?!"

I whispered, "This is the same size table you've been on since you started seeing me."

....

Patient: Obesity runs in my family.

Me: That could be because no one runs in your family.

....

Patient: What's the best weight loss exercise?

Me: Turn your head right, then left. Repeat the exercise every time someone offers you something fattening to eat.

....

While doing a new patient exam, I said, "Stand up and bend sideways and let me know if you feel any pain."

She bent to the side, and I said, "Hmmm, 170 pounds?"

"Huh?" she replied.

"Just taking a stab at it. Do you weigh 170 pounds?" I asked.

"I'm not sure," she said and pointed to the scale. "Why don't you just weigh me?"

"Well, I was going to weigh you, but then I saw the word GUESS on the back of your jeans and decided to take a stab at it."

A patient stepped on the scale and said, "I've gained a lot of weight lately. I think I'm retaining water."

"Nope, it's not water," I replied. "You seem to be retaining food."

Patient: How come I used to be able to eat an entire pizza and not gain weight, but now consuming just two pieces packs on the pounds?

Me: It's your BMI.

Patient: I don't drive one of those, but what does my car have to do with gaining weight?

A patient joked with me that after she entered the food she'd eaten yesterday into her new fitness app, it sent an ambulance to her house.

Me: Do you exercise?

Patient: Yes, I do 365 sit-ups per year. Once each day when I get out of bed.

During an initial exam, I asked a patient to stand on the scale so I could weigh her. I was shocked to see she only weighed 80 pounds! I looked down and said, "Both legs, please."

Patient: I'm so overweight. Do you think my beer drinking could have something to do with it?

Me: Yes, that's why they call it a beer belly. You really should watch your beer drinking.

Patient: So, if I drink in front of a mirror, I won't gain weight?

Patient: Hey, Doc, how can I get rid of my gut?

Me: Crunches.

Patient: I already do crunches daily and that's what got me into this shape!

Me: How is that possible?

Patient: Well, when I eat potato chips, they make a crunch.

A patient came in for a treatment and looked at the scale in the room with mixed emotions.

I gave her a curious look, and she explained, "I'm on a diet and part of the program is that we are not supposed to step on the scale for six weeks. I know I've lost weight because my clothes are loose, but it's only been four weeks." Then she thought about it for a moment and said, "I'm really curious to see how much weight I've lost. I've been so strict."

So, with excitement, she stepped on the scale. I moved the sliding notch to weigh her. It went to 150 pounds . . . then 160 . . . then 180 pounds.

She jumped off. "What the heck?! How the hell did I gain *twenty-five pounds* on this diet?!"

Sensitive to her predicament, I replied, "Let's try it again, and this time I won't step on the scale behind you."

Patient: Hey Doc, I feel like the main character from the movie *Lord of the Onion Rings*. I'm so out of shape that if I were murdered, my chalk outline would be a circle.

A patient says to me, "I've been married twenty years and my husband is just as skinny as the day I met him, but I got fat! When we stand together, we look like the number 10."

A patient pointed to her rear end and said, "I'm hurting right here. What is this called?"

I replied, "That's your gluteus maximus."

She exclaimed, "Is that your scientific way of calling me a fat ass?!"

A man came to see me the day before Thanksgiving complaining of back pain.

I said, "Did you get everything you needed for tomorrow's big meal?"

He replied, "Nope. My wife told me she still needs fatback, which is hard to find at the grocery store."

I grabbed his lower back and said, "I found it!"

PUNNY PATIENTS

WHILE WAITING FOR THE HIGHLY ANTICIPATED 2021 ELECTION RESULTS, a patient wrote on his intake form: "I'm here because I heard on a commercial that if an election lasts longer than 48 hours, see a doctor."

I offered a heat treatment to a patient to help increase circulation and relax his muscles.

"Why do you always put your patients as such a low priority?" he asked.

Confused, I said, "Why do you think my patients aren't my top priority?"

"Because you are always putting us on the back burner."

Patient: How common is lower back pain?

Me: Four out of five people suffer from back pain.

Patient: So, one person enjoys it?

Patient: Dr. Friedman, I just started a new job and I'm really nervous about their 401K.

Me: Why is that a bad thing?

Patient: With my bad back, I can't even run a 5K.

Me: I know you've had bad luck with other doctors, but you can trust me.

Patient: How can I trust someone who talks behind my back?

I asked a patient how he hurt his back and he replied, "I got crushed by a pile of books, but I guess I've only got my shelf to blame."

Me: How did your headaches hold out during all the holidays with your family?

Patient: Well *relatively speaking*, it got worse because my relatives were speaking.

I recommended a neck pillow to a patient, and I explained how it would help *fix* her *cervical* curve. She combined the words **cervical** and *fix* and playfully referred to her pillow as her "cervix."

One day, she walked into my packed waiting room and loudly announced to my receptionist, "I spent a lot of time in bed this weekend, and I think I wore out my cervix!"

Someone let out an audible gasp.

I ran into a patient at the mall one day. "Hey, Dr. Friedman. Congratulations on being voted *Best Chiropractor* in Wilmington."

"Thank you," I said.

"You don't remember me, do you? You have so many patients."

With a puzzled look, I put my hand on her back and said, "Hello, Katy, great to see you again."

With a confused look, she asked, "You had to touch my back to remember who I was?"

I replied, "Of course, I'm your back doctor."

"Well," she said, with both hands on her hips, "thank goodness I didn't run into my gynecologist in the mall!"

"I feel so good coming in to see you, Doc," a patient told me. "You make my EB flow, my YIN Yang, and my ZIG finally go ZAG!"

***

Patient: Do you mind if I take a photo of my X-ray so I can post it on Facebook?

Me: Sure. Why do you want all your friends to see your crooked neck?

Patient: So I can apologize for not believing people when they said my head wasn't screwed on straight.

***

After reviewing a patient's blood work, I told her that her sugar was too high, and she asked, "So, if I move it to the lower shelf, I'll be okay?"

***

I diagnosed a patient experiencing pain in her gluteal area with a psoas spasm. The word is pronounced *sow-ess*. She quipped, "So, the actual medical term of my sore ass is *sow ass*?"

***

I saw a penny on the floor, and I asked the patient, "Is that your shiny new Lincoln?"

The patient responded, "No, I can't afford one. I drive a Chevy."

Patient: Chiropractic is amazing! Your treatments are helping my hair grow by fifty percent.

Me: But you are bald and don't have any hair!

Patient: Yes, I do. I have two small hairs on the very back of my head. Before I started coming here, I only had one.

"Hey, Doc," said one of my patients, "I think I want to give intermittent fasting a try. Any tips?"

"I recommend eating a big breakfast and skipping lunch," I told him.

The next week, when he came back to see me, he said his back pain was much worse since my recommendation. This, of course, concerned me.

"Your back is worse from changing your diet?" I asked.

"No, it got worse from all that skipping at lunch."

Stacy had been using exercise bands to rehabilitate her shoulder, and she told me how excited she was for her upcoming two-week vacation.

"Don't forget to do the bands," I reminded her.

"Oh, Doc, my groupie days are long over."

Patient: I love your book *Food Sanity*. It's right in line with how I've been eating for thirty years. It all just made sense to me.

Me: So, something just clicked.

Patient: It did? I didn't feel anything.

Patient: I'm having surgery on my eyes next week.

Me: Cataract?

Patient: No, I drive an Acura.

A patient was having gut issues and brought her MRI for me to evaluate. I told her the problem comes from the part of the digestive tract called the duodenum.

She asked me to write that down for her so she could tell her husband, then looked at me and said, "So you're saying my problem is that I have two pairs of blue jeans in my gut?"

Patient: I've been hearing a lot about probiotics lately. What do they do?

Me: They help maintain your microbes.

Patient: I'm way too big to be wearing small robes.

I often have a little fun in the office and make a loud pop with my mouth at the exact time I adjust someone's neck.

One day this woman panicked and said, "OH MY GOD, I think you just paralyzed me!"

I tried to calm her down and let her know, "It's not you, it's me."

She replied, "Are we breaking up?"

A patient went to check out at the front desk, and my assistant asked him how he was feeling after his treatment.

He responded, "I feel a lot more like I do now than when I got here."

I've been recommending an herb called valerian root for many years. It's amazing for helping people fall asleep. The only downside is that it has a really bad odor.

One patient told me, "One bottle will last me for a year. I don't need to swallow the pills to help me sleep. I just open the bottle and take a big whiff and the smell knocks me out into a deep sleep!"

Patient: I am going to the beach.

Me: But it's supposed to be bad *weather* today.

Patient: I plan on going *whether or not*.

....

Me: Where are you hurting today?

Patient: I don't want to tell you.

Me: And why not?

Patient: Because you'll mash on it.

....

As I was doing some trigger point therapy to loosen up the muscles, the patient asked, "What are you doing, softening me up for the *kill* before throwing me on the *grill*?"

....

A patient named Kim told me she was eating chocolate for breakfast each day, and I asked her why. She replied, "Well, I'm doing my part as a woman by honoring *HER-SHE!*"

....

Patient: Do you recommend yoga or Pilates to help strengthen my back?

Me: Pilates is much better for your core muscles.

Patient: Oh, I definitely need some help there. I've been told I'm rotten to the core!

Patient: The orthopedic doctor I saw before you said he would have me on my feet in two weeks.

Me: Did he?

Patient: Yes, I had to sell my car to pay the bill.

A patient was using rubber exercise bands to heal from a previous torn rotator cuff injury. She was leaving town to go to a dance competition, and while checking out at the front desk, in earshot of several patients, she said, "I'm going to be getting very physical this weekend, so I'm bringing my rubbers for protection."

I see a lot of people that suffer from hand numbness, especially those who type a lot at the computer. After fixing someone's hand, he referred a coworker to see me who was also suffering from hand numbness.

When he called to make an appointment, he told my front desk person, "I heard from a reliable source that Dr. Friedman gives the best hand job in town."

I was doing some deep tissue work on a patient's sciatica. As he moaned in pain, I said, "Bear with me. I promise you'll thank me when I'm done."

He replied, "Of course, I'll thank you when you're done because you will have stopped hurting me!"

As her appointment wound down, I recommended that a patient lean on tennis balls when sitting to relieve trigger points along the sciatic nerve and to increase blood flow. Because she also suffered from plantar fasciitis (a foot condition), I recommended she roll a golf ball around the arches of her foot.

After her treatment, she went up to the front desk, and with the waiting room full of patients, she shouted, "Darn it! Thanks to Dr. Friedman, I have to go to DICK'S and grab some balls!"

(DICK'S, if you're not familiar, is a sporting goods store.)

I was adjusting Mike, a big construction worker. He said, "Don't let my size fool you. I'm a big baby. Please go easy on me."

While doing some trigger point therapy on his sore muscles, he started to slap the floor three times.

I asked him, "Why are you slapping the floor?"

Mike replied, "I've seen people do that on the wrestling channel, and it made the torture stop."

Me: Are you getting enough exercise?

Patient: Does sex count as exercise?

Me: Yes, sex is considered a great form of exercise.

Patient: Then no.

I was complimenting a patient on how great he was doing and the progress I was seeing. I told him, "I'm proud of you for making your scheduled appointments and following my recommendations on exercising, good posture, and using heat at home."

He replied, "I always give a hundred percent in everything I do in life, except when I donate blood."

An older fellow came in for treatment wearing a Grateful Dead shirt. He said, "Back in the sixties, I used to party like there was no tomorrow. At my age, the only joints I roll now are my ankles."

I was showing X-rays to a patient with a PhD who had a spondylolisthesis. This is a spinal condition that occurs when one of the bones of the spine slips out of place onto the vertebra below it. I told him, "Your X-ray shows you have a spondylolisthesis."

With a puzzled look on his face, he replied, "My X-ray is wrong! I did not do my *thesis* on a *spondylo list*."

Patient: The pain travels into my butt, causing a severe dinosaur reaction!

Me: What do you mean by a dinosaur?

Patient: It's a *lottasorerus*!

Just after eating lunch, a patient's stomach was rumbling and gurgling during her treatment.

I said, "Those sounds are called borborygmi."

She laughed and said, "Nope. I didn't have Greek food for lunch."

I have an elderly patient who has traveled the world. One day, I asked him how old he was.

He replied, "Young man, I was in Baghdad when you were still in Dad's bag."

One of my patients is a ninety-eight-year-old man who is as sharp as a tack. He lives alone and still plays golf. One day I asked him for his secret, and he told me, "I ate a pinecone every single day of my life!" (He loves messing with people's heads.)

Patient: I went to a physical therapist, and I haven't been the same ever since he used that four-letter word.

Me: What did he say?

Patient: OOPS!

A North Carolina senator that I treat really grasped the concept of chiropractic and the physical, emotional, and diet connection needed to attain optimal health.

I told him, "I'm going to call my chiropractic college and see if they will give you an honorary DC degree."

He replied, "It's about time! I visit Washington enough; I've earned the right to have DC after my name."

Me: You have an *acute* case of sciatica.

Patient: I'm glad you think it's *a cute* problem, but it feels ugly to me.

Patient: Dr. Friedman, my back hurts so bad because I work like a dog!

Me: How long have you felt like this?

Patient: Ever since I was a puppy.

One of my patients owns his own website design and repair business. On his intake form, he stated that he was a doctor. I asked what kind of doctor, and he replied, "I'm a U-R-L-ologist."

Patient: What's making this popping sound every time I take a step forward?

Me: Your hip.

Patient: Why, thank you. I think you're pretty groovy yourself.

Patient: My hands have been shaking. What do you think it could be?

Me: Do you drink a lot?

Patient: Nope, I spill most of it.

Patient: On a scale of one to ten, where do I rank as the worst case you've ever seen?

Me: You're an eight.

Patient: No, thanks, I don't have to pee.

Me: That's good to know. You're an eight.

Patient: How am I supposed to urinate if I don't have to pee?

An elderly gentleman was filling out his initial paperwork, and when he got to the question, "Have you experienced a previous whiplash?" he answered, "Yes. At my age, every time I sneeze, I get whiplash."

One day, a patient came in with two prosthetic legs. During his consultation, I asked him how he had lost his legs.

He told me, "I was at a carnival working on one of the rides when the harness came loose, severing my legs. I tried to hire a lawyer to sue the carnival company, but no one would take my case. They told me I didn't have a leg to stand on."

Patient: I was married to a chiropractor once, but we broke up.

Me: Why?

Patient: Because he was too manipulative.

Richard had been to see two orthopedists, a pain management doctor, a physical therapist, and an acupuncturist, but he didn't get any relief.

After his first treatment at my office, he stood up, bent his right leg back, and struck his rear end with his heel. He did this several times. For a second, I thought his leg was spasming involuntarily.

"What are you doing?" I asked.

He replied, "I'm kicking myself in the ass for not coming to see you first!"

I asked a patient how she hurt her back, and she replied, "While doing the Hokey Pokey. I put my right hip in. I put my right hip out, and that's where it stayed."

A patient I had not seen in over a year came in one day and said, "I feel like a library book. I'm way overdue!"

One day, a male patient asked me if Wikileaks was a symptom of an enlarged prostate gland.

I often have patients do rehabilitation exercises for shoulder pain with a rubber exercise band. One day, a woman entered the waiting room and told my receptionist in front of the other patients, "I did the band all weekend, and boy am I sore!"

One guy snickered and said, "It must have been Aerosmith."

Patient: I don't think I need my spine.

Me: Why?

Patient: It's just holding me back.

A patient told me that his neck hurts when he moves it in various directions. I asked him to tilt his head down and tell me what happens.

He replied, "I see the floor."

I was adjusting Margaret's twelfth thoracic vertebra, which sits directly below the lungs, which requires a thrust at the same time as the patient breathes out.

I told Margaret to take a breath in and let it out. The adjustment went perfectly.

She said, "What does taking a breath in and out have to do with anything?"

"The manual thrust and the breathing have to be *in sync* for the adjustment to work properly," I explained.

She laughed and said, "You being a chiropractor, I figured you'd use a *Back*street Boys breathing technique instead of NSYNC."

One day, I held up a life-size plastic model of a spine to demonstrate my diagnosis to a patient, and I said, "This is your spine."

"What the heck?!" the patient cried. "Please put it back inside of me!"

An elderly guy comes in for regular treatments, and it just so happens that he always gets placed in the treatment room right next to the bathroom.

One day, he asked why he's always put in the room closest to the bathroom.

"It's just a coincidence," I said. "But as we get older, it could be a good thing to be close to the bathroom. It all depends—"

He cut in, "Nope. If I wore those, I wouldn't need to make a trip to the bathroom."

I was wearing a new tie, and I asked my patient, "What do you think of my tie?"

She said, "I like a mai tai but I prefer cosmos."

We have a section of the patient intake form that asks, "In case of emergency, who should we contact?" A patient wrote, "911!"

Patient: Wow, I haven't experienced a crack that big since the earthquake I lived through in California!

After a patient's first treatment, he shouted, "Damn. That's gonna leave a mark!"

Patient: I've been having a difficult time sleeping at night. Is there anything you can do to help?

Me: Yes. After today's treatment, you will sleep like a baby!

Patient: Does that mean I'll wake up tomorrow in a puddle of urine, sucking my thumb?

One day a patient told me, "I was going to try physical therapy, but I decided I would give you first crack at it."

Patient: Thanks to you, I have to go buy a dictionary!

Me: Oh? Why's that?

Patient: Because I forgot how to describe a headache. Thank you!

One of my patients was constantly wearing out the sole of his right shoe. I explained this was because his right leg was shorter than his left, so his weight was unevenly distributed when he walked. I told him that once we fixed it through treatment, he wouldn't have that problem anymore.

He smiled and replied, "Dr. Friedman, you are saving soles!"

A patient saw that we offer acupuncture at my office and said, "I'm really leery of acupuncture. The last acupuncturist I went to hurt me with the needle. He was a real PRICK!"

I had just completed an examination on Amelia and told her it was time to get some X-ray pictures of her spine. She said, "Oh, I didn't know I was having pictures taken," as she reached into her pocketbook, pulled out some makeup, and began to apply it. I didn't say anything, but I wondered to myself, if Amelia puts makeup on before an X-ray, what does she do to prepare for a mammogram?

JUST KID-DING

WHEN I TREAT CHILDREN, I try to make it a fun experience for them. Before I do a spinal adjustment, I keep them at ease by explaining, "I'm getting the popcorn out of your back."

One child's inquiring mind wanted to know, "If people stopped eating popcorn, would chiropractors go out of business?"

I told him that I didn't want to find out and hoped people would never stop eating popcorn.

Over the years, my teenage patients have given me quite a few nick-names. My two favorites are "Sir Pop A Lot" and "Crack Master D."

Mother: Nice to see you again, Dr. Friedman. This is my six-year-old son, Alex.

Alex: Is this going to take long? I hope it doesn't take a half hour!

Me: Nope, it should only take thirty minutes.

Alex: Oh, good.

An eight-year-old boy named Jeff came in with back pain after falling off his bike. During my consultation, I asked him what he wanted to be when he grew up.

With a big gleam in his eyes, Jeff replied, "I want to be a fireman!"

When he came back for his second treatment, he was so excited to be there. His mom said Jeff couldn't stop talking about his first chiropractic treatment.

She said to him, "Jeff, now that you've been adjusted, tell Dr. Friedman what you want to be when you grow up."

The little boy smiled from ear to ear and replied, "I want to be a firepractor!"

Last winter, I walked into a treatment room to find a little girl named Amy sitting on my stool. Her mom shouted, "Honey, you need to get off of Dr. Friedman's stool so he can sit!"

Amy dropped to the floor and sulked.

As I sat on my stool examining her mother, I told Amy, "You did such a wonderful job of softening my stool for me. I might just have to hire you."

The smile returned to Amy's face. After the appointment, Amy proudly announced to the waiting room, "Hey, everyone, I'm Dr. Friedman's stool softener!"

Little boy: Dr. Friedman, how old are you?

Me: Well, when I was nine, I was your age.

I did a disappearing pen trick for my patient, Bobbie. After I "pulled the pen out of his ear," his mother told me that he spent the entire weekend asking everyone to look in his ear because he "could feel more pens in his brain." (I don't do this trick for my young patients anymore.)

Ten-year-old Tammy was experiencing lower back pain. After I took X-rays, I diagnosed her with scoliosis.

"Is that hereditary?" her mother asked.

"Yes, it can pass down to other family members."

At Tammy's follow-up appointment, I took X-rays of her mother's spine and went over my findings.

I said, "You, too, have scoliosis. Probably inherited from your daughter."

Tammy began to cry. "Mommy, Mommy, I'm so sorry I gave you scoliosis!"

(I don't tell that joke anymore.)

David's Swiss Army knife fell out of his pocket, and I couldn't help but perform a sleight-of-hand magic trick. The idea is to make it look as if the "cross" logo that appears on the front side of the knife is on both sides.

"Abracadabra!" I said, and using the "paddle twist" technique, I flipped the knife over to create an illusion of the logo on the blank side. Then I said, "Abracadabra!" and tapped the knife—and *voilà*, the cross disappeared. The logo was now only on one side.

After seeing my next patient, I noticed David was still in the treatment room crying. He was scouring the floor for the "second" Swiss Army knife logo that I had made appear and then disappear.

Despite my breaking the magician's code by divulging the secret of the trick, David was *still* inconsolable and demanded I give him back the other cross logo.

(This is a trick I no longer show kids.)

To get to the bottom of seven-year-old Alicia's constant middle back pain, I wanted to take some X-rays.

"I'm so glad you are getting an X-ray," Alicia's mom told her. "Maybe now the mystery will be solved."

"What mystery?" I asked.

"The missing chocolate chip cookie."

With wide eyes, Alicia cried, "Mommy, I told you I didn't eat the cookie!"

"We'll just see about that," the woman told her daughter. "Dr. Friedman will be able to see right through you and tell if you ate the cookie."

Alicia nervously whispered, "Dr. Friedman, will an X-ray really be able to tell whether I ate the cookie?"

"Yes, it can," I said.

That night I went to the grocery store and purchased a bag of chocolate chip cookies. I cut out one of the cookies on the label and taped it to Alicia's X-ray.

The next day, mother and daughter returned. I put the X-ray on the view box and said, "I saw something rather strange, and I'm not sure what it is." I pointed to the abdominal area and explained, "It looks like she swallowed a chocolate chip cookie!"

"Alicia!" her mother shouted.

With a guilty expression, Alicia replied, "Okay, okay! I ate the cookie. I'm sorry, Mommy!"

"You put your shoes on the wrong feet," I told a little boy.

He looked down and wiggled both legs and replied, "Nope. Those are *my feet*."

"S-H-I-T!" a little boy yelled out to the people in the waiting room while his mother checked in. She did not reprimand him, and everyone in the waiting room looked shocked. Once again, he shouted, "S-H-I-T! So Happy It's Thursday!"

A family came in one day with two kids who were all excited about something.

The mom said, "Share the great news with Dr. Friedman. Tell him where you're going this summer."

The older boy said, "We get to go to a Jewish camp this summer. It's called Camp Yimca!"

I said, "I never heard of it, but that's pretty cool."

The mom winked at me and replied, "I think you've heard of it, Dr. Friedman. It's spelled Y-M-C-A."

It was Halloween and a little girl came in with her mom and handed me a bag of M&M's. I said, "Thanks for the W&W's!"

She gave me a weird look and said "Huh? I gave you M&M's!"

I pointed to the bag (upside down) and said, "Read this."

She read out loud, "W&W's . . . Huh?!" She looked at her mom and said, "These are chocolate W&W's!"

I looked at the bag again and said "Oops, my mistake. Thank you for the 3&3's."

She exclaimed, "Huh?!"

I replied, "Yes, read the bag" (which I held sideways).

The little girl reads, "3&3's . . . What?! Mommy these are chocolate 3&3's!"

A mother brought in her ten-year-old whom I had not seen in a couple of years. I said, "Wow, you've grown another foot since I last saw you!"

He looked down and said, "Nope, I only see two."

Before I adjust kids, I always say the disclaimer, "Kids, don't try this at home." Well, little Sammy took what I said to heart. On his next visit, his mother informed me that he went over to a *friend's house* and tried to crack his back.

Because I live in Wilmington, NC, or "Filmington," many autographed celebrity headshots adorn my office wall. One day, a lady came in with her seven-year-old named Nicole. With a big smile on her face, Nicole looked at all the signed celebrity headshots and asked, "Dr. Friedman, did all of these people really come to see you so they could get a photo of *you* to put on their wall?"

I smiled back at Nicole and replied, "Yes, they did. As a matter of fact, many of these celebrities have a signed photo of me hanging up in their living rooms so everyone can see it."

Nicole, beaming from ear to ear, exclaimed, "Wow, they must have been so happy that you signed a picture for them!"

While performing a neurological exam on little Danny, I picked up my rubber tip hammer. He got nervous and asked, "What's that hammer for?"

I replied, "It's to test your *REFLEX, FLE, FLE, FLE, FLE, FLEX.*"

Danny's mom, obviously a Duran Duran fan, started laughing. Danny just scratched his head.

DR. SMITH, WHO'S ALSO A BLACK-BELT IN KARATE, ADJUSTS THE SPINES OF THREE PATIENTS AT ONCE.

Friedman

PRACTICAL JOKES

AN ELDERLY LADY WHO HAS BEEN A PATIENT OF MINE for twenty years was in the treatment room next to the room her son was in.

I asked, "Did you two drive together?"

"What are you talking about?" she asked.

I said, "Your son. He's in the next room."

She replied, "My son comes to see you?"

I became confused and replied, "Yes, he's been coming to see me for over a decade. You didn't know I was his chiropractor?"

She said, "I knew he had a chiropractor, too, but I didn't know it was you."

I asked her if she wanted to play a trick on her son, and she agreed.

I gave her son's chart to her and told her to walk into the room and pretend she is me.

So, she walked into the room and told her son, "Hop up on the table and let's get you adjusted!"

Like a deer in headlights, his eyes popped wide open in shock. He turned bright red and in a little boy voice exclaimed, "Mommy?!"

My longtime patient Bill brought his friend Sam in to watch him get a chiropractic adjustment. Sam had never been to a chiropractor before, so Bill wanted him to see what it was all about. Sam told me that Bill couldn't stop bragging about how good he felt after seeing me, so he'd been looking forward to watching the treatment.

Bill lay on the table, and I flicked him in the ear and then announced, "Okay, we are done!"

We had not pre-planned the practical joke, but Bill played along. He got up from the treatment table and said, "WOW! I told you this guy is amazing. Look how far I can rotate my neck now!"

Sam's jaw dropped, and he said, "All he did was flick you in the ear!"

Bill said, "That's not all he did. Dr. Friedman went to college many years to learn exactly the right angle, speed, and duration to flick people's ears correctly."

I told Sam it was nice meeting him and walked out of the treatment room. I could hear Sam saying to Bill, "But all he did was flick your ear! You pay him for that?"

Bill replied, "Those flicks saved me from getting back surgery!"

Bill and Sam walked out of the treatment room and went up to the front desk to pay. Bill wrote a check, and they left the office. I could hear Sam in the waiting room say, "This guy flicked your ear. It took him less than one second, and you just paid him for that?!"

They went all the way to the car before Bill told Sam it was just a joke. They came back in and I gave him a real adjustment. The three of us couldn't stop laughing. Now, when Bill comes in, he calls me his ear "flickapractor."

My assistant answered the phone, and the person on the other end said, "I need to see all the king's horses and men today!"

"Um, I think you have the wrong number, sir," she replied.

"Nope," he replied. "This is Humpty Dumpty calling. I'm broken and need to make an appointment with all the king's horses and all the king's men to put me back together again. Tell Friedman he needs to bring in the troops!"

A really skeptical patient got his first adjustment and said, "I can't believe it, but I am feeling better. I actually thought chiropractic was one big pyramid scheme!"

"It is," I replied. "You need to go out and tell two people how great you feel, and after they come in and feel good, they have to go out and recruit two new patients, and so on."

Beth had just been examined and brought to the next room to have her X-rays taken. When Beth was finished, she walked to the front desk to check out and realized that she had left her purse in the examination room. By then another new patient had already been put into that room, so I told her I would go get her purse for her.

I walked into the examination room, briefly said hello to the new patient, reached down, picked up the purse, and brought it to Beth.

Beth gave me a strange look and said, "That's not my purse!"

I realized then that I had taken the waiting patient's purse. I went back into the room and said, "We have a new policy to take patients' credit cards so they don't sneak out without paying."

"Very funny!" she said, not falling for it at all, and traded me Beth's purse for hers.

Diane asked, "Dr. Friedman, what do you think of a portable TENS unit? Would having this muscle stim at home help?"

"Well," I replied, "TENS is better than the NINES, but it's become outdated over the years. Just like people update their iPhone every few years, you may want to upgrade to an ELEVENS or a TWELVES unit."

(TENS, by the way, stands for **T**ranscutaneous **E**lectrical **N**erve **S**timulation.)

A new patient was worried about having her neck "cracked" and asked, "You haven't ever broken someone's neck, have you?"

I replied, "You don't have to worry about anything. You're perfectly safe. I only break necks on Thursdays."

She breathed a sigh of relief and then said, "Wait! Today is Thursday!"

A patient said, "I wish you would teach my husband how to do this!"

"I actually offer a free course to husbands showing them how to take care of their wives," I replied. "It takes place all day on February thirtieth."

The patient picked up her smartphone to schedule it into her calendar. "This is odd," she said, scratching her head. "It won't let me schedule for that day."

A new patient named Ed came in wearing a "Class of 1990" T-shirt. In tiny letters on the back of his shirt were the names of people who had graduated from his high school.

As he lay face down on the table, I could read every name. I said, "Ed, do you know someone named Suzie Henderson?"

He replied, "Yes, as a matter of fact, I do. She went to high school with me. How do you know Suzie?"

I replied, "It's a small world. What about Howard Zeinsterson?"

He was shocked. "Yes, I know him too! In fact, he and I ran track together our sophomore year. Does he still have that long beard?"

I replied, "Yes, he does. So much so, he looks like a member of ZZ Top!"

Ed said, "I can't believe Howard is a patient of yours."

I replied, "You would be surprised who I know that you also know. Like Missy Huber and Amy Fitch."

He was completely awestruck and shouted, "OMG! I went to high school with them, too! Who else do you know?"

I proceeded to read some more names listed on the back of his T-shirt. The more people I mentioned, the more flabbergasted Ed became. He went home and told his wife about all the people from his graduating class who also see his chiropractor.

About a month later, Ed came back in for another appointment and was again wearing his "Class of 1990" T-shirt. (I figured it was his "comfy T-shirt," which was perfect for treatment.)

This time I decided to take it up a notch, and I told Ed, "You may not know this, but there's a lady who had a crush on you in high school, but she said you never noticed her."

Ed replied, "Who?"

I scanned the T-shirt for a woman's name I thought I had not mentioned at the previous appointment, "Brenda Rizzo."

He jumped up with his mouth hanging wide open. When I asked him what was wrong, he replied, "Brenda was the prom queen of my high school. I had such a crush on her. I would mumble like an idiot every time I was around her. Did she really tell you that she had a crush on me?"

I replied, "Yes, a big one! She ended up marrying someone else but never stopped thinking about you and what could have been."

That night, when Ed went home, he proudly told his wife that the prom queen of his high school, Brenda Rizzo, had had a crush on him.

She laughed and said, "No way! Who told you that?"

"Dr. Friedman did today, during my appointment."

"Wait a minute!" she said. "Were you wearing this T-shirt at your last appointment, too?"

That's when Ed finally realized I had been reading the names printed on the back of his shirt. At his next appointment, he told me that he and his wife had laughed on and off for hours!

It was the end of the day, and I had one chart remaining. It was a new patient who had written on her intake form under "chief complaint": *Severe, sharp, stabbing pain on the right side of my neck! The pain is killing me!*

I walked into the room and let out a bloodcurdling, high-pitched scream. There on the treatment table lay a dead woman, blood all over, with a knife deeply embedded in her neck. In shock, I immediately ran over to check her pulse, only to discover it was not a real person.

Together with my employees, a special effects team member from the sci-fi/horror flick *Virus* had concocted this elaborate practical joke. The dummy corpse, worth several thousands of dollars, had been used in the film. After my heart rate slowed down, I eventually joined in on the laughter of my entire staff.

A month later, the same guy from the special effects team told me he had jammed his finger while lifting a heavy box and wanted my opinion. He held out his hand, and I could see that his index finger was red and swollen. As I reached to examine his finger, it fell to the ground and landed on my foot.

I jumped back and uttered a four-letter word. For that split second, I actually thought his finger had fallen off. Fool me once, shame on me, fool me twice . . . *shame on me again!*

One day, the local police chief, a patient of mine, walked into the waiting room in uniform. He glanced at the patients and saw me near the front desk.

"Are you Dr. David Friedman?!" he barked.

"Yes," I replied.

"Sir, you are under arrest for operating a crack house and massage parlor." He pulled his handcuffs out and went on, alarming all the waiting patients. "You have the right to remain silent . . . until you adjust my back because I need some crack!"

When the chief and I started laughing, the patients let out the breath they'd been holding and joined in.

Since there is so much fun and laughter taking place at my clinic each day, you can probably imagine what April Fools' Day is like. I've gotten many patients with everything from fake poop in the bathroom to plastic spiders on the treatment table (believe it or not, the men are more scared than the women.) But this special day devoted to pranks is also a time for patients to fool me. Here are a few April Fools' pranks patients have played on me and my staff:

The phone rang and my office manager answered.

Man on the phone: I just picked up a very heavy sack and ran with it. I felt my low back pop and now I'm hurting severely.

Office manager: I'm sorry to hear that. We can see you this afternoon.

Man on the phone: Do you accept cash?

Office manager: Yes, we do.

Man on the phone: Good because that's all I have. After robbing the bank just now, it will be nice to reduce some of the weight in this giant sack of money I have.

Caller: My ass is killing me!

Receptionist: Excuse me?

Caller: I said my ass is killing me! My granddaughter got me the Buns of Steel workout video, and I pulled my butt muscle so badly that I can hardly walk. I can't even sit on the toilet and take a doo doo.

Receptionist: (trying not to laugh) Okay sir. We have an appointment available at four thirty. Would you like to have it?

Caller: How am I supposed to sit in the car when I can't even sit to shit?

Receptionist: Can you find someone that can drive you while you lie in the backseat?

Caller: I have to ask first. Is Dr. Friedman going to have to rub a dub and squeeze my tight butt muscles? I've never had a man do that before.

Receptionist: I'm not sure what Dr. Friedman will have to do until he examines you.

Caller: I'd rather have a woman rub my butt cheeks instead. Can you do that for me?

Receptionist: Um, no, that's not part of my job duties.

Caller: Well, it needs to be your duty so I can take a doodie.

Receptionist: I'm sorry sir. That's not going to happen.

Caller: April Fools! This is Mike Rouse. Got ya!

A long-time patient came in on April 1st and said his ears were ringing and his neck was severely hurting after spending the day at the Charlotte Motor Speedway. He said he could still hear the sounds of the race cars echoing inside his head and he wanted to have X-rays taken to make sure everything was okay. I took two cervical X-rays and when I viewed them, my jaw dropped. There was a miniature race car in front of his upper cervical vertebrae. I was completely dumbfounded! When I shared my findings with him, he busted out laughing, held up a matchbox car, and told me he had it in his mouth when I was taking his X-rays.

FARTS HAPPEN

THE MOST COMMON QUESTION I GET ASKED IS, "Do patients ever fart when you push on their back?" Actually, it occurs quite often during chiropractic treatments. I don't care who you are . . . you fart. Sometimes in the privacy of your own home, and other times nature calls and you have to let it rip in public. But when a chiropractor puts pressure on a person's back, farts happen! While flatulence can be funny (especially to us guys), it can also be a bit embarrassing at times. The responses I've gotten over the years from patients are a gas. Many have made me crack a smile while others just stink! Here are a few memorable post-fart responses I've heard and shared.

Patient: You didn't know I could play "Jumpin' Jack Flash" out of my ass, ass, ass?

Me: Your rendition would make Mick Jagger proud.

"That wasn't a fart, Doc!" Hank exclaimed. "It was my ass blowing you a kiss"!

I had just turned Judy over on her side and gave her lumbar spine a thrust when she let out a loud toot. She immediately screamed at her husband sitting in the corner, "Rick, I told you to stop farting in public!"
He laughed and said, "It wasn't me. The dog did it."

Patient: "Excuse me for tooting. I fart a lot because it's the only gas I can afford!"

After a patient of mine passed wind, he jumped up from the treatment table and said, "Where is your restroom? I think my fart had company."

After a patient farted, he lightened things up with a distraction by saying, "That fart was a blast from the past! Yesterday's burrito."

After Hank let out a doozy he said to me, "It's times like these that I wish I was a giraffe. They never have to smell a fart."

During the pandemic, a patient told me, "I used to cough in public to hide my farts, but since everyone is so worried about Covid-19, now I fart in public to hide my coughs."

After a man farted, he put his right hand to his heart, looked up to the heavens above, and said, "R-I-P"

The second most commonly asked question I get from patients is, "What do you say when a patient farts?" Most of the time, I just pretend I didn't hear it, but if the patient laughs or apologizes after farting, I have to acknowledge that the blast occurred, and I will often add a little humor to ease the situation. Here are a few of the responses I've given to patients after they've farted:

- "Sharing is caring, and I feel the love!"

- "You told me you were a teacher. That sounded more like it came out of a tutor."

- "I better go call the mortuary. Something just died inside of you."

- "There you go again, always talkin' out your ass!"

- "That sounded like two turds fighting. One knocked the breath out of the other."

- "That fart was like a bad student that just got expelled."

- "That sounded like a Piglet fart. He always hangs out around Pooh."

Me: Did you have any milk today?

Patient: Yes, how did you know?

Me: Because that one smelled like dairy air.

Me: Did you eat some onions today?

Patient: No, why do you think that?

Me: Because you just created some serious tear gas!

A pregnant patient accidentally let out a horrendous, foul-smelling fart. She embarrassingly buried her face into both hands and profusely apologized. To lighten things up I said, "You told me you didn't know the sex of the baby. Well, now you do. Based on the smell, it's definitely a boy!" A month later my flatulence theory was spot on. She gave birth to a baby boy.

A deacon of a church came in one day for an adjustment and let out a huge, nose hair-curling fart. He apologized and said, "I'm so glad that didn't happen when I was at church."

I replied, "If it did, you'd be sitting in your own pew."

Patient: (after farting) I think I feel thinner now!

Me: Nope, a fart weighs zero pounds. If it weighs any more than that, you're in trouble.

My favorite comeback after someone passes wind during treatment is, "Never hold in your farts. Otherwise, they will travel up your spine to your brain, and that's where shitty ideas come from."

Me: Dan, you seem really tense. For this to work, I need you to relax.

Patient: Okay.

(He drops his arms to the floor, his muscles go limp, and he lets out a huge fart!)

Me: Dan, when I said to relax, I didn't mean that much.

(Now, every time he comes in for a treatment, I remind him to relax, but not too much.)

After a patient farted, he asked, "Dr. Friedman, can you smell that?"

I replied, "Yes!"

He said, "That means you don't have Covid-19 because you haven't lost your ability to smell. I'll send you my bill for the test."

I had just told a patient to take a deep breath in and let it all the way out as I manually thrust on her thoracic spine. She let out a huge fart and quickly jumped up from the table with a disturbed look on her face and said, "Um, excuse me. I'll be right back."

She then darted out of the room and went into the bathroom. After about half an hour, I realized she had done something a bit more than pass wind. When she finally returned, I didn't know what to say, so I made a promise, "I will never ask you to let it ALL the way out again."

(She never came back for a second visit. News was she moved to a different city so she'd never run into me in public.)

Sometimes it's not patients that fart but me that's to blame for making them think they did. I actually own a fart machine with wireless remote control. Ladies, please don't hate me. It's a common guy thing that I guess I just never outgrew.

One day, I taped the device under the treatment table. An older couple, Henry and Agnes, were waiting to see me. Henry was already lying on the table, and Agnes was sitting on a chair. I stood outside the door and pressed the "fart engagement" button. It let out a loud *pfffttttttt*!

Through the door, I heard Agnes shout, "HENRY! I can't believe you just farted like that! You are such a pig!"

Henry replied, "Oh, I didn't even realize I farted. Sorry about that, dear." (Yes, he apologized.)

I pressed the button again, and this time a wet fart sound echoed from beneath the table.

Agnes exclaimed, "Henry! I told you not to eat that Mexican food last night! Stop it! Dr. Friedman is going to come in and think I farted. If you do it again, I'm gonna slap you!"

Henry once again apologized. I then pressed the "turbo fart" button, and a giant explosive sound filled the entire room.

Agnes shouted, "Okay, that's the last straw!"

I opened the door to find Agnes about to slap her husband. I walked into the room and said, "Hello, folks." I sniffed the air, curled my nose, and said, "Agnes, did YOU fart?!"

With that, she turned red and started slapping her husband on the arm. "See, Henry, I told you he would think I did it."

I quickly let them in on the gag, and they belly laughed so hard that Henry *actually* farted. (I'm not making that up!)

A patient farted, not once, not twice, but three times! I replied, "I guess third time's the charm?"

He made a sinister grin and said, "BUTT wait . . . there's more!"

My eyes started to burn too much, and I had to leave the room.

THE PAIN STARTS IN MY HUSBAND'S LOWER BACK,
THEN IT TRAVELS UP HIS SPINE TO HIS NECK.
THEN IT COMES OUT HIS MOUTH AND INTO MY EARS.
AND THAT'S WHY I GET THESE HEADACHES.

COUPLES COMEDY

I WAS TREATING A LADY WHO ALSO SCHEDULED HER HUSBAND to come and see me for his chronic lower back pain.

During the consultation for her husband's lower back pain, the wife asked, "Dr. Friedman, while you're treating my husband for his back, is there anything you can do to help his snoring?"

"Honey," the husband interrupted, "I told you, I don't snore! I just dream that I'm a motorcycle."

After thirty years of marriage, a divorced patient was heading back to the dating scene. "Hey, Doc," he said, "any pointers on how to pick up women?"

"Sure," I replied, "keep your back straight and lift with your legs."

A patient came in with his wife to witness a chiropractic adjustment for the first time. I adjusted the wife's thoracic spine, and it cracked real loudly!

Her husband immediately fell to the ground and shouted, "Oh my God!"

"Are you okay?" I asked.

He said, "Yes, I'm fine. I was just taking cover. It sounded like a drive-by shooting."

Patient: I'm about to get married for the fourth time, and my head is killing me! Do you have any idea why the thought of getting married causes headaches?

Me: Can't say "I do."

Judy was having sex with her husband, and just as things were getting hot and steamy, she shouted, "Ohhh! I need Dr. Friedman!"

"What did you just say?!" her husband demanded.

"My hip just popped out of place!"

A married couple came to see me and wrote on their intake form: "We are interviewing chiropractors until we find one who's the right fit."

During the consultation, the husband said, "We recently moved to town and have interviewed seven chiropractors that did not impress us. You are number eight on our list."

As I inquired about their primary complaints, I couldn't help but notice that one of my framed diplomas was a little off-center. I got up from my chair to reposition it. "Sorry," I said. "I have a pet peeve about off-center pictures. Sometimes when a door closes in the next room, the frames shift."

The husband smiled at the wife and said to me, "No need for us to look any further. We've found our chiropractor!"

With a puzzled look, I said, "But I haven't even completed the consultation, nor have I started the examination."

The couple exchanged another smile, and the husband explained, "We purposely shifted one of the framed diplomas off-center at each of the previous seven offices—and NOT ONE chiropractor noticed. You, on the other hand, not only noticed it, but you also fixed it."

"What does that have to do with anything?" I asked.

"If you are good enough to notice and fix a misaligned picture frame in your office, you are good enough to find and fix the misaligned bones in our spines!"

I couldn't help but wonder how they'd put a new gastrointestinal doctor to the test. A smudge of chocolate on the baseboard perhaps?

A patient came in with excruciating back pain from a boating accident. She explained, "I slipped off my husband's little white dinghy!"

A man came in one day with nothing written on his intake form—no pain or any symptoms mentioned. When I asked him for the reason for his visit, he replied, "My wife told me to prove to her I wasn't spineless."

Me: Your back is in severe spasm. What did you do?

Patient: I spent all day yesterday bent over, paving roads.

Me: So, it was the asphalt?

Patient: That's right; it was my wife's fault. She's always to blame.

A lady came in with her husband to see her X-rays. The first one I put on the view box was her hip and lower back films. She looked at her husband and asked, "Honey, do these X-rays make my butt look big?"

During a patient's appointment, I was taking his blood pressure, and it was extremely high. I asked him, "Do you have a family history of high blood pressure?"

He responded, "Yes, it definitely comes from my family."

I asked, "Is it your father or your mother's side?"

He replied, "Neither. It's from my wife's family."

I gave him a puzzled look and said, "You can't get high blood pressure from your wife's family!"

He told me, "Yes I can. You'd understand if you ever met them."

A lady came in with back pain after rearranging the living room furniture. She told me that she has OCD and pushes furniture to different locations quite often. After a few treatments, she had full relief under my care. A week later, her husband came in as a new patient suffering from acute back pain. I asked him what happened and he replied, "I got up in the middle of the night to get a glass of water, and on the way to the kitchen I tripped over a loveseat that wasn't there when I went to bed."

Patients often empty out their pockets before lying on the treatment table. Next to a set of keys, a pocketknife (I live in North Carolina), and a cell phone, Stan had a very thin wallet. I said, "Normally I'm having to lecture guys on why sitting on a thick wallet creates a hip imbalance."

He replied, "You don't have to worry about that with me. The only thing I keep in my wallet is a picture of my wife to remind me why there's never any money in there."

A wife brought her husband in to see me and said, "I'm here because I know he won't be honest and tell you what's wrong with him. He's stubborn, pigheaded, and never listens to me!"

I looked on his chart where he had written: "I've been suffering from IDOITIS for 17 years!" I told him I had never heard of that condition.

He explained, "It started seventeen years ago on my wedding day, right after I said *I DO.*"

A not-so-happily married couple came in, and the wife pointed to her husband and said, "He's the reason I get headaches. I get stressed out with all his complaining about all my imperfections. Every day, all he does is ridicule me. He says I'm fat and lazy and I can't cook. He never has anything nice to say, nor does he ever compliment me!"

"That's not true," the husband cut in. "I always tell you how great your hearing is."

Patient's wife: Is it okay if I see my husband's X-rays?

Me: I'd have to get his okay first because once you do, you'll be able to see right through him.

Patient's wife: I already can!

While examining a man with neck pain, I touched his cervical spine and asked him exactly where his pain was.

He replied, "In the corner."

I shifted my fingers lower to the base of his neck and asked, "This corner?"

He laughed and said, "No, that corner" and pointed to his wife, who was sitting in the chair in the corner of the room.

Patient: What does the nervous system do?

Me: It tells the entire body what to do.

Patient: Then I guess my wife is its spokesperson.

One of my patients carries a five-inch-thick wallet in his back pocket. I kept telling him this is what was knocking his hip out of alignment every time he sits.

On the following visit, his wallet wasn't in his back pocket, and I gave him a high five. He saw me a few more times, again, no wallet in the back pocket.

Then, one day his wife came in to watch his adjustment. I told her how proud I was that her husband was no longer keeping the thick wallet in his back pocket.

She turned to him and said, "Oh, so that's why you left your wallet in the glovebox right before we came in today."

A fellow who usually comes to the clinic for treatments with his wife came in one day without her.

"Where's your wife?" I asked.

"We've been spending time apart. I'm thinking of leaving her," he replied. "I'm getting that seven-year itch."

On his next visit, I gave him a bottle of calamine lotion. Just doing my part to keep married couples together.

After I worked on a patient's temporomandibular joint (TMJ) dysfunction for a couple of weeks, there was a great improvement in her jaw pain. One day, she brought her husband in with her to see her treatment.

I said, "You've progressed nicely, and it's time for you to start doing some jaw exercises."

Her husband cut in, "Doc, I don't think she needs more exercise. She already runs her mouth a mile a minute."

The wife of one of my patients called my front desk and asked, "Dr. Friedman has been treating my husband, Tim, for five weeks, and I am calling to find out how much longer the doctor feels I need to keep feeding him breakfast in bed."

My office manager told the woman to hold and relayed her question to me.

I laughed and told her to tell Tim's wife that she should give him a tall glass of milk with his breakfast in bed because he's milking his back pain for all it's worth.

A couple came to my office because the wife was having neck issues. During the consultation, her husband went to the bathroom.

She described feeling worse in the mornings no matter what type of pillow she tried: down pillow, contour foam, and even the My Pillow brand. I proceeded to tell her how to choose the best type of pillow for her neck.

When her husband walked back into the room, I said, "Shhhh! We had better stop all this pillow talk. Your husband will hear us."

One day a woman came in with Band-Aids on her back and told me she had gone to the skin doctor earlier that day to have some tags removed. Her husband sitting in the chair snickered and said, "Now they won't be able to find her in the ocean."

WHAT'D YOU SAY, SONNY?

I WAS EXPLAINING X-RAY FINDINGS TO AN ELDERLY WOMAN, and she kept saying, "Huh? What did you say?"

I realized she didn't have her hearing aids turned up, so I pointed to my ear and said, "Hearing aid!"

She said, "Huh?"

I shouted, "HEARING AID!"

She shook her head and replied, "No thanks, young man, I don't want no lemonade, but thanks for offering."

As I was trying to do an exam, it was obvious that the elderly woman I was treating couldn't hear me. "Can you please turn your hearing aid up?" I asked.

She replied, "Huh?"

I said, "Turn your hearing aid up so you can hear me."

This time she understood and turned both hearing aids up, but now they were emitting a loud, high-pitch sound.

I pointed to her ears and said, "It's making a high pitch."

She replied, "What did you say?!"

I said, "High PITCH!"

She gave me an angry look and replied, "What did I do to deserve being called a bad name like that?"

Patient: I have a hard time sleeping. Is there anything you can recommend?

Me: Yes. Have you tried chamomile?

Patient: How is consuming *camel meal* going to help me sleep better?

Me: It can really help you fall asleep on Wednesdays because that's Hump Day.

I said to a patient, "This is your cervical X-ray . . ."

He cut in, "Huh, what did you say? You'll have to speak up!"

I proceeded to shout during the rest of his report of findings.

A week later he came back for treatment, and I shouted, "HOW ARE YOU TODAY?"

He replied, "I'm doing much better."

I said, "LIE ON THE TREATMENT TABLE!"

After several more shouts, he said, "Dr. Friedman, can I ask you a question? Why are you shouting at me?!"

"Because you're hard of hearing," I said.

He laughed. "I can hear just fine. At my appointment last week, which I came to straight from the airport, my ears were still clogged from the five-hour flight."

Me: Are you prepared for the hurricane they're predicting we will be getting tomorrow? It's already windy.

Patient: No, it's not! Today is Tuesday. Tomorrow is *Wednesday*.

After an adjustment, I told the patient she was done and instructed her to follow me. I walked her to the front desk to check out, and as I turned away, I told her to schedule a follow-up treatment for Monday.

I then headed down the hallway to use the bathroom. As I stepped inside and turned to shut the door, I jumped! Right behind me was the patient. I walked out of the bathroom and escorted her back to the front desk, where I learned she had to read lips because she was hard of hearing. She'd only "read" the words "follow me."

A patient was bragging about his new state-of-the-art hearing aid, which had cost him eight grand.

"Eight thousand dollars! What kind is it?" I asked.

He responded, "Oh, it's a quarter till three."

Me: I see you have heart issues. How is your pacemaker working for you?

Patient: My bladder is just fine.

Me: Huh?

Patient: You asked if my piss maker is working.

Patient: Four years ago, my doctor told me I was probably going to go deaf.

Me: When was your last appointment with him?

Patient: I haven't heard from him since.

POTTY MOUTH

Patient: Doc, I think something's wrong with my bladder; I pee all the time!

Me: It sounds like *urine* big trouble.

Patient: Do many others have the same problem?

Me: Yes, *you're in* the *nation* of frequent *urination*.

Patient: I've been working so hard. I finally have a weekend off.

Me: Are you going to relax and binge-watch something on Netflix?

Patient: No. I don't stream a lot.

Me: That's good because if you did, I'd have to refer you to a urologist.

"I'm having such slow movement," a patient told me.

I replied, "You should try eating more prunes; it will get you regular."

She laughed and said, "That's the number-one funniest thing I've heard all day!"

I replied, "Are you sure it's not the *number-two* funniest thing you've heard?"

I am often asked what makes the popping sound when someone gets their back cracked. It's actually methane gas being released from the joint. So, technically, the sound you hear when you get adjusted is your spine farting. In my profession, we often refer to these sounds as "the fart from within."

One day I told the gastrointestinal doctor I treat, "I would never see you as a doctor."

He looked at me puzzled and asked why.

"Because I saw what kind of vehicle you drive," I replied.

He still looked confused. "What does my car have to do with you not wanting to be a patient?"

"Because you drive a Dodge RAM," I said. "I have issues with someone shoving a twenty-foot tube up my butthole that drives a *RAM!*"

He laughed and told me, "You think that's bad; one of the doctors I work with drives a Ford Probe."

Patient: Wow, that was amazing. You are truly the Lord of Crack!

Me: Nope, that honor goes to my plumber.

I walked in after a patient had just changed her baby's diaper. The soiled diaper was in the trash can, and I could smell it in the air.

When she lay down on the table, I said, "Ewww! You have poo on your pants!"

"Oh my God!" she exclaimed, jumping up and grabbing a tissue from her pocketbook. "I'm so embarrassed! Where do you see the poo?"

I pointed to the back of her pants and replied, "There's poo right there."

When she went to wipe it off, she realized that I was pointing to a Winnie-the-*Pooh* emblem on her back pocket.

She rolled her eyes, laughed, and replied, "I should have known. Only YOU, Friedman!"

A patient who needed to use the bathroom lost his place in the queue.

When he returned and I was ready to see him, he asked, "Why did you put another patient ahead of me? I was here first."

I replied, "In this office, if you poos, you lose."

Me: You have several areas of complaints circled on your intake form. What is your biggest concern?

Patient: I'm concerned with the whole thing!

Me: I'm sorry, you're in the wrong clinic for that *hole* thing. I can, however, refer to you a good butt doctor.

I asked an elderly man where he was having issues. He pointed to his crotch and leg and said, "Tingles."

I replied, "You need to see a urologist if you're having tinkle issues."

After Frank's first adjustment, everything aligned perfectly. I said, "You are going to see a big change after that one!"

He jokingly replied, "Yes, I think I need to change my underwear after that aggressive treatment; I just crapped in my pants!"

There's a technique I do when a patient is tense and won't relax their neck muscles. I take my index finger and gently tickle the side of their cheek and then follow through with the adjustment.

One guy asked me, "That's an interesting way of distracting patients and getting them to relax for a neck adjustment. Is that something you thought of?"

I replied, "Yes, I call it the one cheek sneak. Not to be confused with the other type of one cheek sneak when someone's trying to fart. That's not allowed in this office and tends to tense up people's muscles *and nostrils!*"

An elderly man came in who I hadn't seen in twenty years. After talking to him, I said, "You haven't changed a drop!"

He laughed and said, "At my age, I have to change my underwear because of drops."

Me: Your blood pressure is extremely high. You could have a stroke at any time.

Patient: So, you're telling me I can masturbate whenever I want to? Will you please let my wife know it's okay?

A man came in with very restricted movement in his upper cervical region. I had to do a lot of trigger point therapy before his second vertebra would finally go back into place.

When I was done, I told the patient, "I really had to work for number two today!"

He replied, "You should try eating more fiber."

An elderly fellow came in and after his first adjustment I told him, "That's going to loosen you up."

He replied, "Actually, I think it loosened up a dingleberry!"

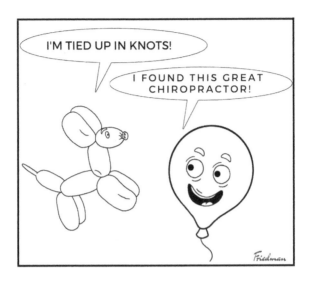

A FEW MORE FOR THE ROAD

AFTER I GRADUATED FROM CHIROPRACTIC COLLEGE, I went to the beach and hung out with Tim, my best friend since I was twelve years old. As we were soaking up the sun, he tapped my shoulder and said, "Dude, check out that beautiful chick in the string bikini!"

I turned my head to look at her and replied, "Oh my! She needs some serious help. She has scoliosis, an externally rocked pelvis, and unilateral metatarsus adductus (pigeon toe)!"

My buddy looked at me like I was a total stranger and replied, "That's what you see when you look at that gorgeous babe in the bikini?"

I replied, "Yes, don't you?"

It was on that day, I realized I would now be looking at women with a different set of eyes.

On the front door of my clinic hangs a sign that says, "Crawl-ins welcome!" And the welcome mat reads: "Welcome. Glad to See Your Back."

Patient: I'm taking cholesterol medication. Are there any side effects I should be aware of?

Me: Yes, some people can experience memory loss. Have you had any issues with a lapse in memory?

Patient: Not to my knowledge.

Patient: Do you have anything you can recommend to help get rid of these wrinkles?

Me: With age comes wisdom. Therefore, you don't have wrinkles. You have wisecracks.

Sometimes I ask patients deep questions to make them think, like:

- "Would you go to someone's funeral if they didn't go to yours?"

- "Have you ever tried drinking chai tea while doing tai chi?"

- "Is today the tomorrow you worried about yesterday?"

- "Want to know what really makes me smile? Facial muscles."

- "Isn't that the same shirt you wore the day after yesterday?"

- "Did Noah include termites on the ark?"

After I showed a patient his X-rays and gave him his diagnosis, along with my recommended care plan, he told me he wanted a second opinion.

I walked out of the room and shut the door.

A few moments later, I opened the door, walked back in, and said, just for a laugh, "Nice to meet you, I'm Dr. Friedman. What can I help you with today?"

Edith arrived late to her appointment and asked if she could use the phone. In earshot of the whole waiting room, she called the church director and said, "I'm going to be late for *choir practice* because I'm at the *choir practor.*"

I've always thought certain parts of the body would make great names for cars:

- Ferrari Testosterone

- Ford Occiput (skull bone)

- Chevrolet Talus (foot bone)

- Honda Sternum (chest bone)

- Porsche Pectoralis (chest muscle)

- Ford Fibula (leg bone)

- Nissan Patella (kneecap)

- Lincoln Lunate (hand bone)

- Kia Clavicle (shoulder bone)

- Nissan Maxillae (jawbone)

- Lexus Lymphatic (immune system)

Patient: What nutritional products do you recommend for improving memory?

Me: You've asked me the same question four times.

Patient: Oh no! It's worse than I thought.

Me: Just kidding. You've never asked me that question before—or did you? I can't remember. I used to have a photographic memory, but then I ran out of film.

Brenda brought her daughter in to get treated for neck pain. I asked the little girl to rotate her head to the right and to let me know if she felt any pain.

As the girl rotated her neck, I heard, "OUCH!" from behind me.

Next, I asked the girl to look toward the ceiling and to let me know if that motion increased her pain.

Again, behind me, I heard, "OUCH!"

This time I turned around. Brenda told me she had been demonstrating the ranges of motion to her daughter. She immediately went up to the front desk to make an appointment for herself.

I was treating a nurse named Llewellyn for two rotator cuff tears. I gave her shoulder rehabilitation stretches to do using rubber exercise bands. I showed her how to intertwine them around the doorknob and do alternating flexion and extension exercises before going to bed and first thing in the morning. She asked me if she could tie the bands around her bedposts and do them in bed. I told her that was a great idea.

One day Llewellyn came in for a visit and told me how embarrassed she was. Come to find out, some members of her church were visiting and while giving them a tour of her house, they noticed the bands tied against her bedposts and exclaimed, "Llewellyn!"

She immediately turned beet red and said, "It's not what you think. I use those for my chiropractor."

The guests' jaws dropped, and someone said, "Your chiropractor!?"

A seventeen-year-old named Sam came in one day looking rather distraught. He said he was having a bad day and I asked him why.

"Well, I went to pick up my date. After her father answered the door, I realized he was the pharmacist I purchased condoms from at the drugstore the day before."

Two of my patients are identical twins. Guess who they look like? Each other.

One day, the twins were receiving therapy while lying next to each other. One of them said to the other, "You know, sometimes I feel like I'm beside myself."

Another day, one of these twins came into the office looking a bit depressed. I asked him why he seemed so down. He replied, "Because my twin brother forgot it was my birthday." I laughed and told him he should go get a drink to celebrate his special day and ask the bartender to pour him a double!

Sometimes I'll slide a patient's chart under the door, usually when kids are in the room to get their attention and elicit some laughter. One day, the mood struck me to do this to a woman and her son who had been patiently awaiting my arrival. I slid the chart under the door, and immediately heard her scream, "Holy crap!"

I went inside. Turns out, the chart had slid all the way across the room and hit her in the foot. She'd just gotten to the part in the novel she was reading where a snake bit one of the characters. But once she realized it was a chart and not a snake that had accosted her, she busted out laughing. Perfect timing like that can only happen once in a million years.

Patient: I've been having memory problems lately. Can you recommend anything natural I can take?

Me: Yes, there are some great herbs you can take for your problem.

Patient: What problem?

A workers' compensation patient came in and told me he was injured on the job and needed to be put on disability. He said, "I can only lift my arm this high." (He raised it to just twenty degrees with a grimace on his face.)

I asked him, "How high could you bring your arm up before you had the injury at work?"

He lifted it all the way up to ninety degrees and said, "I used to be able to lift it this high."

I sometimes do drumbeats on my patients' backs to loosen them up. It's actually a form of Swedish massage called tapotement, a technique consisting of rhythmic percussion movements, administered with the edge of the hand, loose fists, a cupped hand, or the fingers.

Being a drummer, it also gets me in some practice time and offers something fun to do while I'm working. Sometimes I'll play a little game of "name that tune" with patients and do a few beats of a popular song on their back.

One day a man said, "You know, only you chiropractors could get away with playing drums on someone's back. If a dentist, gynecologist, or gastrointestinal doctor played 'name that tune' on the area they work on, patients would run away as fast as they could."

"You're right," I replied, "the day a gastrointestinal doctor does his rendition of the song 'Wipe Out' on my butt cheeks, I'm finding another doctor!"

One of the biggest pet peeves I have is memory foam pillows! They don't correct anything. Instead, they adapt to a lack of the user's neck curvature, offering zero benefits. I always tell patients, "You don't want a memory pillow. It's better to have a pillow with dementia because it won't remember your lousy neck curvature."

There are a lot of great home remedies for back pain. Did you know if you rub a bit of olive oil and Epsom salts on your back, it will immediately feel greasier and saltier?

I called a new accountant that a patient of mine highly recommended. During my consultation, I told her, "I had bad luck with my former CPA, and now I owe back taxes."

She replied, "Don't all chiropractors owe *back* taxes?"

Patient: I've been losing my focus.

Me: Maybe it's time to get rid of your tiny Ford and get a larger car that won't get lost in a parking lot, like a Cadillac.

When I first started practice, I was so busy with patients, I had to work six full days. One morning my wife told me I'd been talking in my sleep. She said I was also pushing on my pillow just as I do on patients' backs right before I adjust them while saying, "Take a deep breath in. Okay, let it all the way out."

She laughed and commented, "Thank God I didn't marry an overworked gynecologist."

Patient: I hear popping and grinding in my joints when I get out of bed in the morning. What do you think it is?

Me: It's called crepitus.

Patient: Are you telling me I'm decrepit?

"At my age," said an elderly gentleman, "my back goes out more than I do. And I hear *snap, crackle,* and *pop* even when I'm not eating cereal."

There's a medical abbreviation I note on anyone's chart if they complain of more than five things: neck, back, arm, wrist, hip, knee, etc. That abbreviation is PPC, and it stands for "Piss-Poor Condition."

A patient made an appointment after suffering from severe back pain after a trip to Disney World. I asked what he thought could have caused it?

"I'm not sure," he said, "but it started after I went on the Tower of Terror."

I replied, "Did you really expect after going on a ride with a name like that you'd leave feeling good?"

Patient: You found exactly where I'm hurting. What is that?

Me: It's your SI joint (sacroiliac).

Patient: How do you spell that so I can look it up on Google? Is it Esseigh?

Me: No, it's S-I.

Patient: Ess Eye?

Me: No. It's the letter "S" and then an "I."

A patient came in with severe back pain after a gym workout. I asked her what she thought could have caused it.

"I'm not sure," she said, "but it started after I took a Body Attack class."

I replied, "Wasn't the name of the class perhaps a small indicator that just maybe your body should avoid it? That's like having jaw pain after biting into a JAWBREAKER!"

I've had several patients over the years who were afraid to get a chiropractic adjustment. But none was ever quite as bad as Mary. During her first visit to my clinic, she was shaking and sweating. In fact, she sweat so much that it drenched the entire treatment table.

Each time I would prepare her for the first adjustment, she would shout, "WAIT! WAIT! I'm not ready. Explain again, what exactly are you going to do?"

For the fifth time, I explained everything. Finally, after thirty minutes of trying to calm her down, I was able to do the adjustments. After each thrust, she would shout, "OH MY GOD! My life is passing before my eyes!"

"It's good to see old friends you haven't seen in years," I joked to lighten the mood.

Mary did not laugh. She left my office physically and mentally exhausted . . . but then, later that week, she returned for her second treatment.

When I walked into the treatment room, she gave me a big smile and said, "I've been looking forward to this!" She eagerly lay on the treatment table and relaxed.

"Who are you and what did you do to Mary?" I asked.

She laughed and said, "Oh, she's right here, but now she knows you aren't going to kill her."

On Mondays, which I call Magic Monday, I do magic tricks for my patients. The kids love it and so do most adults. One day, I was showing a disappearing coin trick to a patient, who is also an OB-GYN.

She said, "I wish you could show me a few of those tricks so I can share them with my patients." Then she thought better of it. "Maybe it's not a good idea for things to disappear from my hands when I'm examining a patient."

One day I walked into a room and saw one of my patients had shaved his head. I grabbed the top of his scalp, squeezed it, and told him to turn his head and cough. He and I cracked up hysterically! His wife was in the room, and she said, "I don't get it. What's so funny?" It's a guy thing.

When I tease patients or tell them a corny joke, they often say, "You know, you're not right, Dr. Friedman!"

I reply, "Nope, I'm not left either. I'm still here."

Patient: You crack me up Dr. Friedman. You are a freakin' nut!

Me: Hey now! I totally resemble that statement.

When I started my practice, a fellow named Barry came in and told me he was hurting in the "small of his back." I examined Barry's neck (the cervical region is the smallest part of the spine). I said, "Everything feels okay to me."

He exclaimed, "That's my neck! I said I was hurting in the small of my back!"

I asked him to point to where he was hurting, and he pointed to his lower back. I quickly learned that in the south, the largest part of the spine (the lumbar region) is referred to as the "small of the back." Who knew? Not I, the back specialist.

Patient: I'm doing something different to lose weight. I've decided to try fasting.

Me: So, you've become a breakfast skipper?

Patient: No Gilligan, I haven't turned into a bowl of oatmeal.

Me: Your X-ray shows one of your hips is higher, which is why you lean to one side.

Female patient: So, what do we need to do from here?

Me: Well, the first thing I'm doing is changing your name on this chart.

Female patient: Why?

Me: Having such a short leg, I'm now going to call you Eileen (*I lean*).

Patient: When would you like to see me back?

Me: Top of the mornin' ole Irishman. I'll have a look-see at yer back again next week.

A lady named Diane came in with surgical Harrington rods in her back after having scoliosis surgery fifteen years prior. On her X-ray, I found two screws that had started to detach from the bone, which is a common finding fifteen years after someone has Harrington rods inserted. I showed her the X-ray and shared my diagnosis, "You have a couple of screws loose!"

Me: Before I do this adjustment on your sore knee, I need to know if you've had any prior surgery on it?

Patient: No. Will I need to after you snap it?

A patient said, "It was a long day. After my adjustment, I'm getting sushi takeout and going home to relax and watch a movie."

I replied, "Are you going to watch *Finding Nemo* while eating your sushi?"

A patient came in and said, "I have a hard time walking downstairs. Last week I fell off twelve steps."

I replied, "So you're back drinking again?"

One day I was adjusting a patient and there was a hollow sound. I asked, "You must not have had breakfast this morning because that sounded hollow."

He replied, "As a matter of fact, I always skip breakfast."

I commented, "Then my nickname for you is Hollow. Yes, Hollow be thy name!"

An older fellow named Stuart came in wearing a shirt that said "POPPY" on it with several hearts around it.

I asked him what his shirt meant, and he told me his kids call him Poppy and they got him that shirt for Father's Day.

I replied, "So that means all your children came from Poppy seeds."

A lot of patients ask me why I became a chiropractor. I've known it was the career I wanted to pursue since I was a child hooked on popping bubble wrap.

Lori was in a lot of pain and said to me, "I hope you give me a fantastic treatment today; I really need one."

I noticed the headrest paper roll was almost empty and jokingly said, "The patient who lies on the last piece of the paper roll always gets a fantastic treatment."

After her adjustment, Lori stood up and exclaimed, "Wow, I feel so much better! That's the best my back has ever been popped!"

A week later, Lori came back in for a follow-up treatment, and I noticed the trash can was filled to the top with headrest paper and there was just one small piece remaining on the roll. This was odd because I had just replaced it with a brand-new paper roll earlier that day.

With a smile on Lori's face, she said, "I'm lying on the last piece of the headrest paper again, so I know I'm going to get another fantastic adjustment today!"

Vince from New York came in to see me. He had a very sore neck. After I did some deep manual therapy on him, he said, "I was a Yankee when I got here but I'm leaving your office with a *red neck*!"

After not seeing a patient in a while, his adjustment created a very loud pop.

I said, "That's been out for a long time!"

He replied, "Yep, has been!"

I replied, "Don't call yourself that. You are not a has-been. There is still hope for a better future."

Female patient: I did not sleep good, period!

Me: That's not good. What about when you are not on your period? Do you sleep better those three weeks of the month?

In my city of Wilmington, NC, we've been unfortunate to have been hit by several devastating hurricanes over the past couple of decades. One day, while Hurricane Fran was heading our way, a patient who was wearing a *Star Wars* shirt had just finished his treatment, and I said, "May the force be with you!" Probably not the best thing to say to someone when a Category 4 hurricane is approaching.

There's a painful condition called gastroesophageal reflux disease, commonly referred to as GERD. It occurs when the acid from the stomach enters the esophagus, which causes severe heartburn.

A new patient came in and asked me if I had ever heard of GERD. I replied, "Well-a everybody's heard about the GERD. G-g-g-gerd, G-gerd's the word. Everybody knows that the GERD is the word."

(Younger readers, don't fret if you don't get this. It's sung to The Trashman's hit song "Surfin' Bird" from the '60s.)

A patient came in really sore at his twelfth thoracic vertebra, which is the segment right above the lumbar spine.

He asked, "What is that bone?"

I replied, "It's T12, your transitional segment, where the thoracic region segues into lumbar spine."

He asked, "So is this transitional segment part of the LGBTQ community?"

Patient: Hey, Doc, my wife joined a local plant-based eating group in town.

Me: I belong to that group too, but I've never seen herbivore.

It was July of 2015, and temperatures were in the high nineties. A new patient named Alan came in to see me for treatment of lower back pain. When I walked into the consultation room, his body odor was so bad that my eyes watered. After he left, the stench continued to linger through the hallways for hours!

The next day, he came back in for treatment and his body odor was even worse! Patients complained to my office manager that they would not make another appointment unless they were assured it wouldn't be during the same time that Mr. Stinky was scheduled. I didn't know a polite way to tell Alan that his odor was causing patients to complain. So, I decided to try using a friendly, subtle approach.

I *attempted* to adjust his back but told him that his muscles were way too tight for me to get any movement. I recommended that he take a hot shower or soak in a bathtub before his next treatment. Two days later, Alan returned, and once again, the horrendous smell of putrefied rotten eggs lingered through the entire office. I again attempted to adjust Alan's back with only minimal movement.

I said, "Alan, your muscles are still too tight. Did you take a hot bath or shower as I recommended?"

He replied, "No. Do you really think it will make a difference?"

I assured him that it would. Two days later, Alan returned for treatment and there was no odor at all. On that day, I gave this man the best chiropractic adjustment of my entire career. Bones moved like never before!

Alan exclaimed, "Wow! I felt the adjustment that time! I took your advice and soaked in a bathtub. It really works."

He continued to come in for subsequent treatments and no one's nose hairs ever curled up again.

A woman came in and told me, "My head hurts so bad, it feels like it's separated from my neck!" I asked her how long it had been feeling like that, and she told me, "Two years."

I replied, "In North Carolina, after being *separated* for a full year, it's legally considered a *divorced* neck."

A new patient came in named Richard Aberdee. After I adjusted him, I wrote on his chart and headed toward the door.

He said, "Are we all finished, Doc?"

Using my best Porky Pig impression, I replied, "Aberdee aberdee aberdee, that's all folks!"

ACKNOWLEDGMENTS

A RECENT GALLUP POLL FOUND THAT MOST PEOPLE feel dismissed or ignored by their doctors. They just don't have the time or interest in bonding with and getting to know their patients. Twenty-five years ago, I worked on the cast and crew of the Golden Globe Award–nominated film *Patch Adams*, starring Robin Williams. It was then I would learn about an amazing doctor that brought friendship and laughter to his practice. Patch showed me early in my career that it was okay to loosen up my tie and combine humor without compromising my skills as a doctor. Fast forward to 2022 and I had the honor of interviewing Patch on my radio show and thanking him personally for inspiring me.

And, of course, this book would not have been possible without all the wonderful patients that have graced my life over the years, many of whom are now like a part of my family. When a patient enters my clinic, I have one mission. I want them to leave with a smile. Sometimes that goal is accomplished after I give them a pain-relieving treatment, while other times it requires performing a magic trick or sharing a funny story. And there are some days when a patient simply needs someone that they can vent to that will truly listen to them and cares. Whatever it takes, when a patient smiles, it enriches me in all four chambers of my heart.

And finally, I want to sincerely thank all my wonderful employees that have greeted every patient with a smile. You are the patients' first and last impression and have always cheered them up when they walked in and made them look forward to returning when they leave. You are the epitome of stellar customer service. Teamwork makes the dream work and because of you, I have enjoyed the practice of my dreams.

ABOUT THE AUTHOR

DR. DAVID FRIEDMAN is the international award-winning, #1 national bestselling author of *Food Sanity: How to Eat in a World of Fads and Fiction*. He's a chiropractic neurologist, doctor of naturopathy, and clinical nutritionist. He received a post-doctorate certification from Harvard Medical School, is a board-certified alternative medical practitioner, and is board certified in integrative medicine. He's a former teacher of neurology and author of the college textbook *Understanding the Nervous System*. In addition, Dr. Friedman is a contributing writer for a plethora of leading news, health, and fitness magazines, including *U.S. News & World Report*, *Newsweek*, *Readers Digest*, *Better Nutrition*, *Woman's World*, and *Forbes*, just to name a few.

The Hollywood Reporter calls Dr. Friedman "The chiropractor to the Stars" because his clients include many of today's top celebrities. As the health expert for Lifetime Television's syndicated morning show and host of *To Your Good Health Radio*, millions have enjoyed his knowledgeable yet entertaining approach to solving everyday health and wellness issues.

Dr. Friedman's holistic health clinic has been honored in the *National Who's Who Directory for Distinguished Businesses* since 2002, and his memberships include:

- American Chiropractic Council on Neurology

- Institute for Functional Medicine

- Naturopathic Medical Association

- American Dietetic Association

- American Association of Drugless Practitioners

- American Holistic Health Association

- Academy of Nutrition and Dietetics

- Academy of Integrative Health & Medicine

- Foundation for Chiropractic Education and Research

- American Nutrition Association

- Nutrition and Dietetic Educators and Preceptors

To learn more visit: DrDavidFriedman.com